Your AI Survival Guide

Scraped Knees, Bruised Elbows,
and Lessons Learned from
Real-World AI Deployments

Sol Rashidi

WILEY

Acknowledgments

To my dearest mom, husband, and children who have all sacrificed and ensured I never bore the burden of guilt for business travels or for the countless hours dedicated to work and this book. Your unwavering encouragement allowed me to focus and finish every endeavor I ever started.

Mom, your belief in me and support at home, with the kids, and the family is truly appreciated. I can never repay you; I only hope as a daughter I've made you proud.

Drew, you're my number-one champion, confidante, and the rock who grounded me through all my adventures. You shouldered extra burdens with the kids and our home, a haven of warmth and support. Thank you for being such a supportive and caring husband.

To my amazing children, your adaptability and resilience inspire me. You've never complained or made Mommy feel bad; you've embraced my dreams with open arms and hugs.

A special thank-you to a few key folks who, throughout my career, have been with me through thick and thin, have helped me with professional transitions, or have given me the opportunities to think big and prove the art of the possible. Thank you, Jay Bellisimo, Jay Schneider, Lisa Caldwell, Sin Leung, Mitch Modell, Joe Reis, Jepson "Ben" Taylor, Owen Rogers, Carl Haney, Arpa Gupta, Guy Kawasaki, Kenyon Brown, Richard Fain, Adam Goldstein, and Margarita Sullivan.

About the Author

Sol Rashidi is an esteemed executive, leader, and influencer within the AI, data, and technology space. Having helped IBM launch Watson in 2011 as one of the earliest world applications of artificial intelligence and having completed more than three dozen large-scale implementations, she is at the forefront of ideation, conceptualization, design, and development of data and AI applications. Sol has 8 patents granted, and has received the following awards:

- "Top 100 AI Thought Leaders"
- "The Top 75 Innovators of 2023"
- "Top 65 Most Influential Women"
- "Top 10 Global Women in AI & Data"
- "Top AI 100 Award"
- "Global 100 Power List"
- "Isomer Innovators of the Year"
- "Top 100 Innovators in Data & Analytics"
- "Chief Analytics Officer of the Year"
- "Chief Data Officer of the Year"

- "50 Most Powerful Women in Tech"
- "Forbes AI Maverick of the 21st Century"
- "Top 100 Women in Business"

Sol is an energetic business executive skilled at coupling her technical acumen with storytelling abilities to articulate business value with start-ups, scale-ups, business owners, private equity firms, and Fortune 100s that are leaning into data, AI, and technology as a competitive advantage, while wanting to preserve the legacy in which they were founded upon.

Sol has served as a C-suite member across several Fortune 100 and Fortune 500 companies, including the following:

- SVP, Chief Analytics Officer—Estee Lauder
- VP, Chief Data & Analytics Officer—Merck Pharmaceuticals
- EVP, Chief Data Officer—Sony Music
- VP, Chief Data & AI Officer—Royal Caribbean Cruise Lines
- Partner - Ernsty & Young—Ernst & Young
- Partner leading Watson Go-To-Market—IBM

Sol is now an advisor, consultant, global keynote speaker, and fractional CDO and CAIO helping companies advance their business objectives. Her hallmark is to make the complicated uncomplicated and to help business leaders realize not everything needs to be cutting edge; sometimes innovation comes from cutting through the noise.

Contents

Foreword		**xi**
Chapter 1	**Overcoming the Inertia**	**1**
	Inertia	3
	Who Is This Book For?	5
	Organizational Benefits	6
	Business Benefits	7
	Business Growth	8
Chapter 2	**The Rogue Executive**	**11**
	Why the "Rogue Executive"?	12
	My Formative Years	14
	Sports	16
	Leveling Up	16
	Coach Doug	17
	My Transition to Artificial Intelligence	18
	Joining the C-Suite Ranks	21
	Where Rubber Meets the Road	23
Chapter 3	**Bend the Rules, Don't Break the Spirit**	**25**
	The Framework	26
	Ask "Why?"	27
	Develop Your AI Strategy	28
	Think Big, Start Small, Scale Quickly	30
	Choose Your Technology Partner	31
	Pace Yourself	32
	The Five Pillars	35

Chapter 4	**How to Start**	**37**
	The Experience You Need	38
	Framework for AI Initiatives	41
	Phase 1: Conducting a Readiness Assessment	43
	Readiness Questionnaire	45
	Questionnaire Results	51
	Phase 2: Your AI Strategy	55
	Demonstration of How It Works	60
	Phase 3: Creating and Selecting Use Cases	61
	Use-Case Ideation	61
	Use-Case Selection	63
	How to Score Criticality and Complexity	64
	Real-World and Practical Walk-Through	69
	Phase 4: Preparing and Designing	72
	The Vision	74
	The Impacts	76
	The Approach	78
	The Process	84
	The Support	89
	Phase 5: Selecting a Solution	91
	Tool Selection	92
	Interoperability with Your Experts	97
	Phase 6: Deploying and Going Live	99
	Key Outcomes	101
Chapter 5	**Your Project Killers: The Wrong People**	**105**
	Change Ain't Easy	105
	Team Virtues	107
	The 10 AI Archetypes	110
	The Naysayer	111
	The Evangelist	111
	The Doer	112
	The Discerner	112
	The Blind	113
	The Curmudgeon	113
	The Saint	114
	The Optimist	114
	The Data Scientist	114
	The Know-It-All	115
	Change Management	115
	The Dumpster Fire	118
Chapter 6	**Human in the Loop**	**123**
	What is "Human in the Loop"	124
	Responsible AI	124
	The Four (4) Layers of Responsibility	125

	The Six (6) Tenets of Responsible AI	128
	Transparency	128
	Accountability	129
	Fairness	130
	Privacy	130
	Inclusiveness	131
	Diversity and Nondiscrimination	132
	Human in the Loop	132
	My Nightmare	133
Chapter 7	**How AI Will Impact Every Industry and Function**	**137**
	The Tipping Point for AI	138
	How AI Is Impacting Various Businesses	139
	Blue Chips	140
	Well-Off Private Companies	140
	Small Business Operations	141
	Start-Ups and Scale-Ups	141
	Small Businesses	142
	How AI Is Impacting Industries	143
	Agriculture	143
	Travel and Leisure	145
	Manufacturing	145
	Retail	146
	Media and Entertainment	148
	Healthcare	149
	Consumer Electronics	150
	Fashion and Apparel	151
	Education	152
	Food and Beverage	153
	Environment Health and Safety	154
	Conclusion	155
	How Artificial Intelligence Is Changing Functions	155
	Legal	156
	Procurement	156
	Project Management Office	157
	Human Resources	158
	Customer Service	159
	Sales	161
	Training and Development	162
	Finance	163
	Research and Development	164
	Marketing	166
	Conclusion	167

Chapter 8	**AI Jargon and Development**	**169**
	What Is AI?	169
	What Is *Not* AI?	171
	The Difference Between Artificial Intelligence and Human Intelligence	172
	Jargon, Terms, and Definitions	173
	Computer Science	173
	Data	176
	Analytics and Data Science	176
	AI Terms	178
	How We Got Here	182
	Early 20th Century: Conceptual Foundations	183
	Mid to Late 20th Century: Expansion, Growth, and Challenges	184
	Late 20th Century: Rapid Growth	185
	2010s–Present: Modern AI	187
	Conclusion	189
Chapter 9	**What the Future Holds**	**191**
	What Keeps Me Up at Night	194
	What's Next	197
Appendix: Sources		**201**
Index		**205**

Foreword

Forget the buzzwords and ditch the hype. You hear *AI* everywhere, but what does it *really* mean? Is it robots taking over the world or something more practical?

As a seasoned tech entrepreneur and former NASDAQ space company CEO, I've seen my fair share of trends come and go. But trust me, AI isn't a fad. It's here to stay, and understanding it is crucial for anyone wanting to stay ahead of the curve.

That's where Sol's book comes in. Forget about dense technical jargon. Sol is a rare breed: someone who can explain complex concepts like AI in a way even "mere mortals" like us can understand. Think funny stories, real-world anecdotes, and practical advice, all rolled into one engaging read.

Here's why this book stands out:

Cuts through the BS: Sol separates fact from fiction, giving you a clear picture of what AI is and what it can (and can't) do.

Actionable insights: No more theory! Sol provides practical steps for deploying AI solutions in different industries, showing you how to put this knowledge to work.

Down-to-earth approach: Even if you're a tech newbie, Sol's relatable stories and humorous writing style make you feel like you're having a conversation with a friend, not a tech guru.

Whether you're a CEO, entrepreneur, or just curious about the future, this book is for you. It's not just informative; it's fun! Think of Sol as your guide on an exciting journey into the world of AI. Trust me, you won't regret taking the plunge.

Dive in, explore, and emerge with a clear understanding of the AI revolution. Sol has got your back.

Richard Greco
Former NASDAQ CEO

Overcoming the Inertia

"In a world that thrives on conformity, standing
apart tests your resilience."

—Sol

I'm no Elon Musk or Peter Thiel. I'm not a Sam Altman (CEO of OpenAI) or even close to the geniuses who created neural networks or Watson and DeepMind. I'm not here to preach or prosecute on all the glories of artificial intelligence (AI), nor am I here to give you a technical dissertation on its intricacies. I'm not an academic or researcher, nor do I get paid to write code or promote vendors or tools.

I'm simply a practitioner who worked her way up through the corporate ladder—one who worked relentlessly with blind determination not knowing exactly where her career would go, one who eventually made it to the C-suite as the Chief Data Officer, Chief Analytics Officer, Chief Data and Analytics Officer, and Chief Data and AI Officer for many Fortune 500s, one who accidentally fell into the world of data in the early 2000s and into artificial intelligence in 2011 when I helped IBM launch Watson.

I never thought that doing AI deployments, I would face so many unexpected challenges, but the reality is that you can take a licking along the way because transformations involve change, and well. . .people are generally averse to change. This is why I have the scraped knees, bruised elbows, and wounded pride from my experience in real-world deployments. Over the years I've tried multiple approaches, implemented numerous strategies, and have had countless alignment discussions selling, convincing, aligning, conceiving, designing, deploying, training, monitoring, and measuring the successes and failures—trying to figure out the art of AI deployments and how to balance the messiness with the possibilities. The approach I share with you in this book is practical and realistic, and it's based on real failures and successes where I've captured the lessons learned over the years.

I believe in the "crawl, walk, run" approach because I've seen what happens when you try to run without crawling first. What I will share with you is very pragmatic and grounded. There will be no selling or advising on anything that pushes you too far, and nothing in this book is based on theory, heresy, or academia. I will be realistic with you about what artificial intelligence can and can't do (right now), and I will help you sift through the hype.

This book is intended to help you start your AI journey and succeed, while familiarizing you with and minimizing the friction points that I have experienced. Many books you read will mention that you need a strategy, you need to pick a use case, you need data, and you need governance. I will outline for you, step-by-step, how to select a strategy, how to ideate, and how to select a use case, and I will provide you with an "essentials lists" rooted in real, roll-up-your-sleeves work.

I know how to do AI deployments because I've had the tenacity to take on early, unproven, and questionable projects that disrupt the status quo. I think and do things differently, and I'm perfectly fine with pushing boundaries and pushing people who lack imagination. Building the reputation of a "rogue executive," I developed intuition, an innate ability to see the "art of the possible" and the "art of the practical." This, combined with my relentless pursuit for progress and need to make an impact, has brought me to this point. It wasn't easy; it came with many sleepless nights where I doubted myself.

Furthermore, where I am today in my career has nothing to do with how I started my career. I was in sales at first and then became a project lead. At one point I was even a financial advisor for Morgan Stanley (Series 7 certified and all). Somehow in the early 2000s tech found me, and I pivoted. The real change occurred, however, when I helped IBM launch Watson in 2011. I fell in love with AI and have been doing deployments for some very prominent companies, since.

I'll be the first to tell you I'm technical but not a "techie." I'm business minded but not the president of a Fortune 5 company. What I am, however, is an executive who doesn't mind rolling up her sleeves and getting into the details while also playing a strategic thought leader. I can pivot quickly between the two worlds. I pride myself on having an entrepreneurial spirit and pushing boundaries where few have the energy. Over the years and through the trenches, I've built a backbone versus relying on a wishbone. I'm not afraid of the work or the challenges, and I stay grounded in my successes because I believe you're only as good as your last innovation.

With that, I will pass onto you the knowledge I've gained over the years. This book will give you real frameworks, techniques, how-tos, and approaches to make your AI journey a success beyond the hype of what you have read elsewhere. It's grounded in experience and from someone who has not been afraid of the work.

While some executives focus on self-promotion and preservation, I've focused on trying what most don't dare to do. I hope you like reading what I'm about to share!

Inertia

Like riding a bike, some things must be done before you can learn how to do them. You can read all the books and manuals you want, but nothing prepares you better than jumping in, trying, falling, and trying again! This is how AI is done. This is how life is done! AI is not a silver bullet! It's not a light switch that turns on! It is not a magical solution nor a quick fix. In fact, it can uncover some unpleasant realities about your business, its operations, your employees, and larger issues at hand.

I've been a business leader in the AI game since the days when flip phones were cool. From triumphs to face plants, I've seen it all. Learning AI for business? It's just like learning to ride a bike. It seems wobbly and impossible at first, but once you start pedaling, the most difficult part is done.

As mentioned earlier, I transitioned from a no-name project lead to an established C-suite executive (four times over) and fell into this space accidentally. I didn't study computer science or mathematics, and I sure can't write sophisticated code. However, I learned the ways, and you can too.

This entire book is crafted for you if you're:

- A business leader wanting to explore the benefits of AI without all the messiness and failures I've had to go through
- A business owner who thinks it will benefit the organization but don't know where to start
- A practitioner who wants to make a case for AI but doesn't have the experience of developing a strategy.

- A person who just wants to get into AI but doesn't know where to start
- Someone curious who just wants to be informed and educated about how it's done

Regardless of your role and reasons, just know that 70% of the success of your AI deployment has nothing to do with the technology. As a matter of fact, the tech is the easiest part of the lifecycle. Most of the work is dealing with human capital and relationships, aligning with goals, overcoming fears, picking the right strategy, picking the right use case, and finding the ambition, the energy, and the rogue in you.

It's also important to note that this book is not a guide or a manual for:

- large technology-based companies that are already deeply involved in AI innovation,
- nor is it for the researchers who are shaping the future of cognitive computing and machine learning.

Instead, it is a call to action for business leaders, business owners, practitioners, and the curious, who serve companies where technology has played a supportive role rather than a leading one. This book will be your compass and serve as your call to action.

There will be less emphasis on technical know-how and more emphasis on business acumen. Together we will explore the different types of AI deployments and how they will amplify and accelerate your everyday work, regardless of your maturity.

As you progress through the book, consider each chapter as a building block. The book is structured in a way to discuss different facets of deploying AI in the following manner:

- Chapter 2 is about leadership and finding the rogue executive within you. You must dare to be different to do this! There's a memoir of how I got started; I share with you my story so you know my humble beginnings and gain confidence in knowing that if I did it, you can too.

- In Chapter 3, we'll progress into some key principles I learned along the way about bending the rules but not breaking the spirit. It's focused on how to introduce AI into your company by following these steps: 1) asking yourself why you want to do this; 2) learning to pace yourself through better forecasting; 3) thinking through a strategy; and 4) thinking big, starting small, and scaling quickly.

- Chapter 4 is where we get into the weeds of things. It's long, it's detailed, and it will walk you through every step of an AI deployment. I felt getting into the details early in the book would be of value to you.

- Chapter 5 is about knowing your biggest project killer: your team. We will discuss how to build one from scratch and how to work with people you've inherited. We'll talk about the virtues you want in people on your team, as well as the 10 AI archetypes of people you will consistently have to deal with but may not want to.

- Chapter 6 is about making sure that your AI deployments have a "human in the loop." This is about avoiding or creating any negative impressions or press internally, and externally.

- Chapter 7 gets into inspiration. I share with you 60 use cases, three across 10 industries and three across 10 functions, to help you become knowledgeable about what's happening in the space. The goal is to educate, but mostly inspire you. The world of AI and its experimentation is big, so I've consolidated a list to save you time on research.

- Chapter 8 is about AI jargon and its history. This chapter helps you understand the difference between machine learning and descriptive analytics. This foundation will then help you identify what is and is not AI; along with the evolution of the technology and how we got here.

- We then end with Chapter 9 on what the future holds and where we're headed. It also contains a wrap-up of key takeaways and essential lists.

Who Is This Book For?

As mentioned earlier, this book was written for business leaders, business owners, practitioners, people who want to get into AI, and the curious. Whether you're a C-suite executive, a mid-level manager, a data practitioner, working at a small company, or working at a large enterprise that is not tech-based, this book was written for you if any of these descriptions sound familiar:

- You work for or have a business that currently does not lean on technology as the primary product or service.

- You're in an industry that's legacy-based (i.e. transportation, insurance, brokerage firm, etc.), and bare-minimum tech was good enough until now, but you're expected to make investments and don't know where to start.

- You're a business owner who has made it based on great marketing, relationships, and your network, and now you need to "level up" to stay competitive and relevant.

- You have business pressures to increase profitability, improve consumer experience, increase personalized touch points, produce higher conversions, etc.

- You work for a company, and you fear your job will be replaced by AI, so you want to upskill, versus resist the movement.

- You're curious and want to learn how AI is shaping the world, but you need it described in approachable and non-techie terms.

- You are a small or medium-sized business owner who wants to do more with technology.

- You are an enterprise C-suite leader who is not a technologist and need to learn the practicalities of this space and how it may impact your domain.

- You are an AI practitioner who needs to educate your boss or is often asked how to approach AI.

- You want to get started in the AI space, but it's currently not connected to your career path.

Who this book is *not* for?

- You're in AI and work for a tech-based company like Google, Meta, or OpenAI.

- You're in deep research for an academic institution like MIT or Caltech.

Organizational Benefits

As a person new to this world, it's natural to think "Is it worth it?" or "Why go through all this effort?" This is especially true if things are fine the way they are. The simple truth is, if you don't, your competitor will. It's simply a matter of time. Staying relevant is a tough game. Putting in place practices that will maintain or grow your market share, increase your profitability, lower your cost of consumer acquisition, and enable efficiency and productivity is just good business practice. Whether you strive for growth, quality, or both, AI is a great solution.

By taking your first real step into exploring AI, it will do the following:

- Force you to look at your business processes and operations in ways you haven't before. You will discover core issues, not symptoms, that plague your day-to-day work.

- It will surface naysayers and those afraid to change from those who will help you evolve. You get a great view of your workforce and their attitude (and aptitude) toward change.

- You quickly identify those who are resilient and those who fold at the first sign of an obstacle. You need more of the former and less of the latter.

- It will test your own character and the type of leader you are. Are you cut out for leadership, and will you do whatever it takes to sustain and thrive?

- Do you have a growth-based mindset? Are you willing to act and not just talk about the future?

- It will test your ability to stay positive for your own well-being, your teammates, and your partners. Being known as "cheerfully resilient" (a term used to describe me during my Royal Caribbean days) is key. This stuff is hard, so how you react when trying something new will be observed by many.

Business Benefits

In addition to the organizational benefits, there are many business benefits. The business case for AI is that it gives business leaders and practitioners the information and resources they need without consistently relying on head count and investments as your typical business practices. You'd be amazed at how well it can help you accelerate, facilitate, and amplify your workloads and business processes with better consistency and quality. What's not to love? If you're still not convinced in overcoming the inertia of starting your first AI project, maybe this will help:

- AI has proven to improve the productivity of 61% of employees.

- Agents who use AI can handle 13.8% more customer inquiries per hour.

- Business professionals who use AI can write 59% more business documents per hour.

- Programmers who use AI can code 126% more projects per week.

- 54% of organizations state that AI has been a cost-effective measure for their business operations.
- Netflix claims to have saved more than $1 billion annually using machine learning from its Netflix Recommendation Engine.
- AI helps you become more efficient, allowing you to maintain and control head-count growth, as market demands fluctuate.
- AI is great for capex investments. It allows you to make investments in an asset that can bring you long-term value.
- Your company stays relevant, allowing it to maintain its competitive advantage within your industry and local communities.
- You're taking a proactive step in evolving the business, which teaches your workforce the disciplines of adaptability, change, and thinking bigger.
- You're strengthening and testing your leadership abilities for yourself and the organization.
- You learn to do more with less. It's about working smarter, not harder.
- It's only a matter of time before your clients ask you about AI. You can speak the truth only if you've done the work. As a result, you're distinguishing yourself from your competitors and proving to be a better partner for your clients.
- If you have children, nieces, or nephews, it'll allow you to stay relevant and "cool." Heck, they may even ask to come intern for you. Mad respect!
- You will have better mastery over the politics of big projects. As brutal as the experience of failure is, the process of building teaches you a host of lessons.

Business Growth

And if all that isn't enough, here are some statistics of the space and its anticipated growth:

- Eighty-three percent of organizations worldwide claim that AI is a top priority for their business.
- The AI market is expected to grow twentyfold by 2030.
- The AI market in the United States is expected to reach $299.54 billion by 2026.

- Due to the adoption of AI, the global GDP rate will grow by $15.7 trillion by 2030.

- The year 2024 is set to see the rise of 8.4 billion AI-powered digital voice assistant units, which exceeds the total global population.

- Since 2000, investment in AI start-ups has grown 6 times. Goldman Sachs predicts the investment in artificial intelligence to soar to $200 billion by the end of 2025.

- Gartner estimates that about 80% of enterprises will have used generative AI API's and models by 2026 and/or deployed generative AI applications in production environments.

- The industry value of AI is projected to rise by 13 times over the next 7 years, which is good news for AI-oriented businesses in 2024.

- More than 80% of executives from the retail and consumer industry plan to use AI automation for their businesses by 2025.

- China will be the world leader in AI technology with 26.1% of the global market share by 2030.

- With an exponential surge in revenue from an estimated $86.9 billion in 2022, the AI market is poised for extraordinary expansion, expected to reach an astounding $407 billion by 2027.

- By 2030, 1 in 10 vehicles will be self-driving.

- The global revenue of the AI software market is currently more than $100 billion.

As you can see, the expansive growth of AI is not just a trend but a fundamental shift touching every aspect of our lives and the broader business ecosystem. The journey into AI offers more than just organizational and business advantages; it's a critical step in maintaining your market position and ensuring personal and professional relevance in the changing landscape.

So, I implore you to start now and not be afraid to overcome the inertia.

Remember, every expert was once a beginner. I started from humble beginnings and am now a translator between the business world and the technology world. You'll have the advantage of leveraging my 25 years of business experience, 20 years of technology experience, and 14 years of AI experience in the real world. I will share with you the lessons learned so that you can be successful and reduce the learning curve of what's to come.

Happy Reading!

The Rogue Executive

I've been in the business world for 25 years, in the technology world for 20 years, and in the AI world for 14 of those 20 years. My lens is very pragmatic, grounded, and uncomplicated as I grew up from humble beginnings. A child of immigrant parents with no wealth or last name to open doors for me nor, good looks or charm to carry me through, I had no choice but to lean into my stubbornness and extreme fear of mediocrity to carry me forward.

With that as my foundation, and a few pivotal career moments, I stepped into this world and built a reputation over the years. Some positive, some negative.

- I'm a businessperson who is a technologist that speaks "plain English" when strategizing, planning, designing, and developing capabilities across a variety of functions and industries.

- I'm a rogue executive. I never fit into any corporate culture or tribe. I learned to be comfortable with that, and eventually confident with it, and realized my role was to push boundaries and people so popularity wasn't my priority, my job was my priority.

- I'm a person who learns from failures, unfortunately.

- I have served many industries and many functions, so I have a broad perspective of companies, regions, markets, and organizational cultures.

- I push people past their comfort zone; some love it, others not so much.

The next few pages give you a closer look as to my humble beginnings and how I started. I decided it was important to share this with you. Why? Because I think it will build your confidence in taking the first step of your AI journey. If not that, it will at least give you a few laughs.

Why the "Rogue Executive"?

Why am I a "rogue executive"? Let's start with a snapshot of the past few years of my professional career, and then we'll pivot into my earlier professional years. This will help you understand how things came about and how all the stories, anecdotes, and suggestions connect.

To start, I joined the C-suite ranks early in my career because of my knowledge of data and artificial intelligence, both of which became "hot" in the mid-2000s. I am grateful of, and appreciate of, every opportunity, every leadership team, and every company that has hired me and took a chance with Data and AI as a strategic initiative.

In 2016, as one of the first newly appointed CDOs of the world, I opened the ranks and started the role of the Chief Data Officer (CDO), Chief Analytics Officer (CAO), Chief Data and Analytics Officer (CDAO), and Chief Data and Artificial Intelligence Officer (CAIO) when I got my first C-suite break.

In addition to my technical acumen, it also helped that I had great storytelling abilities, which made it easier for the business to see and feel the innovation I was speaking of; my narrative resonated well with most (if not all). I built relationships quickly, and I was able to bring the business along for the journey if they had the maturity to see what I saw.

One could think, "All this sounds great, so what could go wrong?" The short answer is, nearly everything! Throughout all my roles and titles, I struggled. I struggled a lot. Why? Because what I was doing was new and different, so I faced objections, naysayers, people who lacked imagination, or individuals who didn't want to work harder than their 9-to-5 jobs.

I faced constant resistance and barriers due to people and culture; it drained me of both energy and inspiration. I was constantly in the business of selling internally because of the great divide between aspiration and perspiration. Here are themes I consistently witnessed across corporate culture:

- Companies had the desire to transform and innovate but always got in their own way. They struggled to clear the pathway for new hires to innovate, so retention was an issue. They also didn't pass along mandates to evolve, making it more of a grassroots effort, which never works with legacy-based industries.

- Companies had the desire to leverage AI to differentiate themselves, but they were not making the needed investments in infrastructure, data, or talent or making their strategic intent clear.

- Companies had promised their board that "data was a corporate asset" and "AI was a strategic priority" but had overcommitted to too many things, and other competing priorities were getting in the way or people were stretched too thin.

To make matters worse, I personally felt isolated, misunderstood, and even ostracized at times because no one understood my space. So, while I was driving the agenda of the shiny new object with the board of directors, I was constantly competing for time, attention, focus, and funding.

Unfortunately for them (and me), I was also stubborn and never quit. Going back to my swimming, water polo, and rugby days, quitting was never an option, and pushing past the barriers, the pain, and the resistance was the norm. Little did I know, I would need it in my professional career. To sum it up, my competence and personality got me hired, my relentless pursuit in persuasion got the company started, and my determination got the company past the finish line, but always at a cost.

- I had to exchange popularity for progress, and by corporate standards, this wasn't always good.

- I was going rogue to corporate culture. Going rogue doesn't mean you're purposely going against the grain to be difficult; it's just that you are charged with a mission to change and innovate, so you must naturally be bold, progressive, and different.

- You see the world in a different way and what could be. As such, you're having to constantly evangelize the benefits, stay positive when others don't believe, and manage your frustrations because some weeks or months feel like Groundhog Day.

Now, if you add in the fact that I'm a child of immigrant parents (so I'm not privileged or entitled), combined with the grit and resilience that's been developed over the years of playing sports, I naturally have a different approach. Giving up when times are difficult is simply not an option.

I've also developed the muscle for how things should look, not how they look. I'm not a futurist or anything; I haven't lost my marbles, but I can see the possibilities and put effort in realizing them. I can't count how many times teammates have come back to me after I've left a company only to say, "Sol, remember that thing you said two years ago? Well, it's actually happening now, and people are starting to see it." My favorite was when a former vice president told me in conversation that "Anna" had publicly said, "Sol was right about a lot of things." For context, Anna was a person who made my life hell. Even though I was an executive at a Fortune 100 company, she would reprimand me in meetings for not filling out an Excel spreadsheet the way she had asked. She would question my delivery frameworks and models, not from a place of curiosity or experience but from a place of doubt when she didn't have a lick of deliver experience. So, to hear her say "Sol was right about a lot of things" was simply validating.

All this is to say that "doing AI" is not a technology problem; it's a people problem and a mindset problem. It creates obstacles only a rogue leader can overcome. Over time, naysayers don't discourage rogues, and failures don't scare rogues. What scares rogues is mediocrity and not creating the value that they know can be achieved.

That is what AI deployments are all about: seeing what others cannot and working past what others reject. You need to find the rogue in you to do that.

My Formative Years

I never fit into any clique growing up. I operated mostly as an underdog and often underestimated. I never had a tribe or a community; I wasn't pretty, I wasn't a jock (although I did play sports), I wasn't a rebel, I wasn't an academic, and I wasn't a gamer. Growing up in the 1980s and 1990s, these were some of the classic high-school archetypes (as depicted in the amazing movie *Breakfast Club*), and I wasn't any of them.

I was quiet. I listened to my elders, feared being reprimanded, and never disrupted the status quo. This is now ironic considering how I developed into a rogue executive.

To make matters worse, I never wanted to draw attention to myself because of the criticisms I received for my ugly looks and weird name.

I grew up in a small town called Yorba Linda in Orange County, California. We moved from Los Angeles because every immigrant parent wants the best for their kid, and my parents' version of "best" was a safe neighborhood, decent schools, and a place where kids would stay out of trouble.

From the time we moved there, it was clear: we were not the typical family. Everyone was blond-haired and blue-eyed; we were not. I was an immigrant girl who escaped the Iranian Revolution in 1978 named Solmaz Rashidi. Can you imagine growing up with a name like that when everyone in your class is either Jennifer, Rachel, or Melissa? Ugh! Also, since kids couldn't say my name, they often called me "Hey you" or "Fat Girl." Sometimes I even got a racist name, but usually I wasn't familiar with those terms, so they never bothered me.

It wasn't until second grade that I actually got a name, a real identity. My second-grade substitute teacher went through roll call, calling out names: "David (here), Michael (here), Sarah (here), Jennifer B (here), Jennifer D (here), Jennifer S. (here), Melissa (here), S. . .S. . .Sul-miz?" I assumed that was me, so I said "Solmaz," its phonetically sounding. My substitute teacher looked at me silently saying, "Are you serious?" He paused, waited, and then said, "You're Sol from now on." He simply just chopped off the last three letters, and "Sol" it was. I've carried that name since second grade, and it's a part of who I am today.

With my new name, I had a new identity. I was Sol—the shy, fat, hairy, Middle Eastern girl. Elementary school, middle school, and high school were awesome, primed for someone who looked like me.

Next came academics. When you're an ugly duckling until your early 30s, there's not much else to do but study. Still, I was an average student at best. I worked hard to consistently get Bs. I survived elementary school and went unnoticed in middle school—all successes in my book.

Then came high school, the first game-changer in my life. I started freshman year without a hitch. Then one day my mother came out of the blue and said, "You're fat. Go join the swimming team."

In case you don't have any Middle Eastern friends, this is very normal talk in our culture. We are not woke. "You're too skinny," "You're too fat," "That looks horrible on you" are common feedback. Persian parents and friends aren't worried about the sensitive nature and psychological well-being of their children; what doesn't kill them makes them stronger is the theme. Their view is each generation is much more privileged than the previous one, so it's a rite of passage to be cruel.

While I liked the idea of sports and my mother was somewhat right, I wasn't an athletic person. After all, we're Persians. Persians in the United States don't play sports. The only thing we consider a sport is driving our BMWs in the middle of LA traffic while closing a deal, shifting gears, and taking notes. We are masters of multitasking, not sports.

Sports

To lose weight, my mother suggested swimming. There was just one slight problem: I didn't know how to swim. I mean, I knew how not to drown, but I didn't know how to swim. So, when tryouts came, I showed up in my two-sizes-too-large Kmart swimsuit. Why? We immigrants had to save money and buy sizes we could grow into, not sizes we already fit into. I had no goggles, and I had my long, shaggy hair in a scrunchie. The coach and the kids looked at me in horror when I showed up.

Long story short, when tryouts were done, I was still struggling to finish my first lap. Needless to say, the coach blew the whistle and asked me to get out of the pool and had me sit on the bleachers. She asked why I was trying out for the swim team. We talked. The coach for some reason understood and had sympathy for me. She said, "Sol, you're a horrible swimmer; you're not even a swimmer yet. But I can teach you. Do what I tell others during practice and then stay an extra 30 to 60 minutes afterward, and I'll teach you technique." So I did. After all, I had no social life. What else was I going to do?

Fast-forward three-and-a-half years, I was competing in state championships for 50-yard butterfly. Me, basic old me, the underdog went from nothing to something. Why? I didn't quit. The early seeds of a rogue were in me, and I just needed the experiences of life to bring them out.

Leveling Up

There are times in your life when you're tested, and if you pass, you level up.

When I joined the swim team, I was surrounded by smart, athletic guys and gals. I'd be lying if I didn't say I was the dumbest and slowest one on the team. As I became integrated into the swim team though, I started studying them, and adopting their ways. My grades went from straight Bs to having some As, then mostly As, and then straight As. Nothing had changed except who I surrounded myself with.

As a business leader, business owner, executive, peer, teammate, or practitioner, you quickly learn that who you surround yourself with has the greatest impact in your life. It's the number-one factor in shaping your present and future. Think of how teenagers pick up languages and habits from their friends. It's the same for us too. Leveling up is about the crowd and company you keep. If you're running a company full of naysayers or complacent teammates or, worse, find yourself surrounded by people who lack ambition, you're going to be as good as they are. Change your environment immediately! Your length of imagination and abilities will go only as far as the company you keep.

So, "leveling up" is about not limiting your own beliefs; it's about overcoming any apprehension that gets in your way by surrounding yourself with people who push you past the point of comfort. This is what Doug did for me.

Coach Doug

By the end of my senior year, things were looking good. I went from being an overweight and awkward Middle Eastern girl to a scholar athlete who swam in state champions and played water polo on a boys' team. Yes, a boys' team!

Title IX hadn't gotten wide implementation yet, so for any sport where there wasn't a women's team, we got to play on the men's team. In my case, I enjoyed swimming, but I *loved* water polo. There was a goal, a purpose, and a team comradery that was unmatched. The only problem was that there wasn't a girls' team, so the only option was to join the boys' team. This was problematic on many fronts.

- We played in men's tournaments, so women's locker rooms were closed. I learned to "deck change" like the boys. This is tougher for us gals since we have more body parts to cover. I'm sure the boys got to see more than I would have liked, but thankfully no one ever commented on it.

- Boys are stereotypically taller, so they have longer arm spans, which means more speed and more power. As such, I had to work twice as hard to even compete.

- Some boys tried to get fresh with me under water, grabbing places they shouldn't. After all, all was fair in love and war, and I'm the one who chose to play on a boys' team, so I thought it came with the territory. I didn't expect any sympathy.

- My speed and strength were underdeveloped compared to the guys, so I stood out as the slow poke.

- Finally, Coach Doug was *livid* that he had to deal with me. I was slower than the boys and a waste of time for him. Coach Doug tried breaking me on many occasions. His strategy was, if he couldn't kick me out, he'd try to get me to quit. I honestly think my teammates were nice to me because they felt sorry for me. But as with most things, I didn't quit. I loved the sport, and I enjoyed my teammates. There's nothing like adversity to bring the rogue out in you.

I trained five to six hours a day and, over time, developed my abilities to becoming an average athlete on the men's water polo team. It turns out, a girl with average abilities on the men's team is a great athlete on a women's team. A tape of me playing was submitted to a college recruiter, and a few months later, I was accepted to play Division 1 water polo for Cal Berkely. I didn't get a scholarship or anything fancy like that, but I was recruited to play water polo, and everyone was happy for me, including Coach Doug.

I loved Berkeley. What an amazing experience! I joined a sorority, I played water polo, I majored in chemistry (don't ask me why), and I experienced true freedom for the first time in my life. I was out from under the watchful eye of my parents. Eventually I left water polo to play women's rugby and met my friends for life. I loved rugby too. There's nothing like playing a sport and purposely being asked to be tackled to prepare me for the career that was to come.

My Transition to Artificial Intelligence

Now how does one transition from rugby to artificial intelligence, and how does it all connect to what is being shared with you in this book? Well, after graduation, my first real job exposed me to the world of data. Not knowing what I wanted to do, I took on a variety of jobs from selling servers for websites (data) to being a certified financial advisor (all data) to becoming a project lead delivering basic tech projects (more data). However, the transition that really forced me into the field of "data" was a random situation.

I joined a small LA-based company as their head of business development. We sold tech talent to companies on a full-time or part-time basis, what we now call staff augmentation or professional services. The job was mostly comprised of gathering requirements, negotiating rate cards, and finding the talent. It was great exposure. I learned a lot about different types of technical roles and how skill sets and certifications translated into capabilities. At the time, my CEO had a relationship with a Fortune 50 CIO. That company was going through a major system upgrade, and we were one of the vendors that would potentially provide them with resources. After two months of working on the deal, the CIO told us he couldn't give us any part of the deal because we were a small agency without any clear distinction.

I assumed we were losing the deal and redirected my energy toward other clients. That's when my CEO pulled me aside and said, "We have a game plan to win the deal." Apparently, my CEO and his friend, the CIO, had a "chat." This chat would change the trajectory of my life.

If we all think about our life and the twists and turns it's taken, there are moments we can point to that set the stage for greater journeys. It could be getting a new job or promotion, going through a marriage or divorce, moving to a new city, starting your own company, choosing to stay in your current company. Whatever it may be, there are moments in our lives that sets the course for something else, something that's much bigger. Here's where my speck happened.

My CEO said, "Sol, you're going to Dallas, Texas, for six weeks to be Master Data Management (MDM) certified. This is a hot area right now, and no one in Accenture has this expertise. The course starts in three days. If you pass this exam and get MDM certified, we get the deal, but if you fail, you're fired."

What? What just happened? At the time, I could barely spell MDM. I had no idea what it was nor how it played into the overall deployment of this company. Typical me, I was up for the challenge, so I went to Dallas for nearly two months. I attended class every day afraid that I wouldn't pass. When exam day came, I threw 100 "Hail Marys," took the test, and waited to get the results one week later. I passed. I was now officially 1 of 11 people in the world certified in MDM. How did this happen?

My CEO shared the good news with the CIO, and we got the contract but one catch. I had to be the MDM lead on this $100 million system upgrade. I had never led a team or a technical project, nor did I know what master data was outside of whatever I learned in the six-week course. To make it more awkward, I was being billed at $400/hour, one of the most expensive consultants on the project.

Nearly a year into the project, my name started floating around the Accentures, IBMs, Deloittes, and KPMGs of the world, and they came knocking, wanting to recruit me.

That's when I joined IBM in 2008 as an MDM lead. This was by far the deciding moment of my career. I owe everything to IBM. IBM gave me the start I needed. I started out as a practitioner, being told where to go and what I needed to do. My goal was to deliver and sell more services through delivery excellence. Clients loved me although my teammates hated me at times. I pushed them. I challenged them. I wasn't showing up to work 70% or half-engaged. I had been given the chance of a life-time, and I wasn't going to take it for granted, so I showed up every day at 110%. I was called "intense" by many—a label given to us women who have a clear point of view and expect deliverables to be completed on time and with quality. The rogue in me continuing to strengthen.

Over time I found my tribe at IBM. We were a motley crew of data, business intelligence, and SAP platform experts, and we all loved what we did. We showed up 100% for our clients. Eventually we all went from being leads to leading teams, leading projects, and selling $50–$100 million deals. We all became Partners, and I walked out of IBM with patents. I got to travel the world, solve different data problems for different clients, and be exposed to nearly 60+ Fortune 500 companies across a variety of industries and functions. That experience was priceless. I learned how to present, how to have executive presence, how to sell, how to deliver, how to manage, how to innovate, how to solve problems, and how not to get overly stressed. I learned it all at IBM, and I *loved* it!

Then two monumental things happened. In 2011, Watson beat Ken Jennings on *Jeopardy*, so IBM made the decision to take Watson to market as the first commercial AI platform sold (B2B), and Ginny Rometty became the first female CEO of IBM. Wow! What a year.

What happened to IBM after that was crazy. My boss's boss went to Watson, and I followed him. I pretty much begged at first, I won't lie, but everyone knew you couldn't do AI without data, so it made sense to have someone like me on the team. I also knew this was the moment to break free and get into something different. There was another frontier to be explored, and I wanted in! That was the beginning of my AI journey.

In 2011 I joined the Watson team, and learned about product development, engineering, use-case identification, prioritization, deployment strategies, what worked, what didn't, why company culture mattered with early innovations, why some use cases worked for some clients and didn't for others, how to start a project, and what questions to ask. The failures, successes, scraped knees, bruised elbows, disappointments, excitements, and a slew of other experiences were all rolled up into a single experience at an amazing company.

To this day, I still don't think IBM gets the credit it deserves with Watson. Think about it: Watson was the first commercialized AI product that was enterprise-grade. Its first product, Engagement Advisor, was leveraging what we call *generative AI* today. It was a user interface that leveraged natural language processing (NLP), powering the interaction between the computer and user, and sat on top of a big data ecosystem.

Back then, no one was better positioned than IBM to create the first AI product. Why? IBM was one of the few businesses in the world that had enough compute, storage, and workload capabilities. With these capabilities, it had the first-mover advantage.

As such, I learned how to deploy complex delivery projects because of the four years I spent doing MDM deployments at IBM, and I learned innovation at scale because of the four years I spent doing AI deployments at IBM. During my time at Watson, the use cases varied. We developed intelligence systems in the form of virtual agents that helped financial advisors provide better recommendations for a financial strategy. We created knowledge stores for customer support so that when customers called about a product or had a question about their warranty, they weren't relying on memory or institutional knowledge to recall the facts.

Fast-forward to 2024, 13 years later, we're still discussing, designing, and developing those same uses cases for commercial banks and customer support teams. These are still the most popular use cases globally today. Go figure.

Joining the C-Suite Ranks

With the experience of Watson, I quickly learned that failure builds character and resilience. I learned innovation is messy, and pushing past barriers isn't as easy as textbooks make it out to be. That's why I'm not a big fan of theory or heresy. You really have to do the work before you understand the intricacies not spelled out in frameworks.

After IBM Watson I decided to spread my wings. I wanted to gain more experience and continue my work in AI but for companies where technology was not at the core of their business. I felt I could have more impact. I joined Ernst & Young (E&Y) as a Partner in their Digital & Transformation Division. Royal Caribbean, the cruise line, was one of my first clients. I loved them. Nearly eight months into my job at E&Y, Royal Caribbean asked me if I would join their leadership team, and in 2016, I joined them as their Chief Data and AI Officer. We debated, however, if Chief Data and Cognitive Officer would be more suitable since *AI* had a negative connotation in 2016 after the rise and demise of Watson. The term *cognitive* was more popular and replacing AI.

Regardless, in 2016 I joined Royal Caribbean full-time as their Chief Data and AI Officer, a title my COO and I negotiated while I was four months pregnant and moving to Miami.

Some have said I was the first Chief Data Officer appointed in Corporate America, and others claim I was the first appointed Chief Data and AI Officer. It was a title that in 2023 has started to permeate the corporate ranks.

Regardless of my title, role, and scope, my experience at Royal Caribbean was wonderful. The company is amazing, and in looking back, it's my favorite employer to date. We did some remarkable things there, and they were willing to experiment.

After Royal Caribbean, I joined Sony Music as their Executive Vice President and Chief Data Officer. That was a fun industry. I got to meet a lot of great people and had a few starstruck moments.

After Sony Music, I joined Merck Pharmaceuticals as their Chief Data and Analytics Officer, although that was a short stint. My tolerance for harassment of any kind had shrunk to zero, so like always, I exited gracefully.

After Merck, I joined Estee Lauder as their Chief Analytics Officer. That was a fun company, and I had a terrific leader.

All this is to say, I've had some great roles, big responsibilities, and bigger lessons.

However, my biggest lesson in life was learned when I transitioned to the C-suite ranks of Corporate America. I learned my success depended less on my intelligent quotient (IQ) and more on my emotional quotient (EQ), business quotient (BQ), and social quotient (SQ). I had to master common sense, speak "plain English" (and not technology lingo), articulate business value, and make everything we did about the businesses we served.

Honestly, I sucked at it at first. I was never taught, trained, or told that EQ, SQ, and BQ were equal to, if not more important than, IQ in the political battle ground of Corporate America. I also learned how different industries operate, how different functions function, what motivates executives (their bonuses or the greater good), and that only 30% of the workforce does most of the work.

I also learned that nearly 70% of my time was spent on aligning, evangelizing, and selling the innovation where investments were needed to get the job done. This was a far stretch from where I had come from.

I learned that corporate culture is the number-one determining factor in how well companies evolve, innovate, and advance. By innovate, I mean have the audacity to ideate, conceptualize, design, develop, and adopt the innovation knowing that at the first sight of setbacks or challenges, they won't stop. This is innovation: pushing past the exhaustion in the pursuit of something bigger. This is rare to find in corporate culture. Why? Stock prices, earnings per share, and market perception of company value are what pays executives and employees. Innovation and incentives were in direct conflict.

I eventually concluded that my job was inherently flawed. Why? Because while companies hired me to drive change, I was going against corporate culture and would be judged for it. I was the rogue executive whether I wanted the title or not.

Where Rubber Meets the Road

To clarify, when I use the term *rogue*, I don't mean defying "the man" or going against the machine and being difficult for the sake of being difficult. A rogue is one who perseveres in the face of adversity. When most people quit, get tired, or have excuses for why something didn't happen, rogues push forward. In my experience, it happened with school, swimming, water polo, MDM, and Watson. Your experience will be different of course, but I'm sure you've had moments like this if you're reading this book.

Whether you're the business leader who didn't quit in the face of adversity, you started a company without experience, you built a product based on an observation, or you have a burning desire inside of you, you've got the rogue in you as well. This will set you apart because you have ambition. This is why I'm putting so much emphasis in finding the rogue executive within you.

Furthermore, you'll need this rogueness because when deploying AI projects, you'll face resistance because of the fears people have about losing their jobs. As rogue leaders, you must keep the confidence, strength, motivation, and tenacity to deal with the resistance and disrupt the status quo for the sake of longevity and competitive stance.

As such, this book was written to help you! I want you to achieve success when disrupting the status quo. It is not just a guide on how to start your artificial intelligence journey through my experiences, but a story about embracing your inner rebel, defining who you are as a leader, and showing up in service of others because you believe it's the right thing to do, regardless of what people say and how they feel about you. You'll need those reminders when you take on your first AI project. Everything can be navigated if you're prepared, and this book is intended to prepare you.

In summary, while the intention of this chapter wasn't to talk about me per se, it was meant to give you context as to who I am, how I got here, and my approach toward life. It doesn't come from a sci-fi novel or deep research in a technical area. I'm a normal person from humbling beginnings who's been embedded in the space of AI for a while and approaches things in a pragmatic way. I have the scraped knees, bruised elbows, and wounded pride that come with the hardships and gains that AI can bring. I'm here to help you explore and deploy AI successfully so that you can inspire, innovate, and encourage others to think differently.

I want you to embrace artificial intelligence and learn how it can help you. Identify the rogue in you, and then take a chance and transform as the world around us has. Today, business leaders and practitioners are the new-age rebels, so, whether you're the business leader, business owner, manager, teammate, practitioner, rebel, maverick, or rogue, dare to be different, and always have the courage to be yourself and embrace the change that's here to stay.

Now that the foundation has been laid, let's get to the good stuff. Let's begin our journey into the how-tos!

CHAPTER 2

Bend the Rules, Don't Break the Spirit

In Chapter 1, we touched upon the journey of an underdog, consistently underestimated yet cheerfully resilient. This helped me grow into the rogue executive, pushing boundaries to help companies transform. To say I was constantly faced with roadblocks is an understatement. Yet with a keen eye for what the future could hold, I stood the course and grounded myself with the belief that what I was doing was in the best interest of the company, and this helped me push past the naysayers, the Karens, and the Richards of the corporate world, and boy were there a ton of them.

In this chapter, we'll discuss the five key principles I've learned over the course of my career. This is part of your preparation before we get into the meat of things. They are:

- **Ask "why?"** Make sure you know why you want to do this.

- **Develop your AI strategy.** We start thinking through your strategy.

- **Think big, start small, scale quickly.** This is a framework for making sure you take a "crawl, walk, run" approach to your AI journey.

- **Choose your technology partner.** Like with anything else in life, who you chose as your partner in this journey can influence your experience.

- **Pace yourself.** I share with you how to forecast your project and preserve your well-being.

In the realm of effective leadership, we're often confronted with the inevitable business decision of how to strike balance and adhere to established rules, while calling out when traditional methods and rigid protocols are no longer serving the business. This balancing act is fundamental to both personal growth, organizational success, and staying relevant with changing times. As a result, you learn to bend some rules.

While bending the rules sometimes requires defiance to push past fabricated boundaries, it should never come at the cost of breaking our spirit, well-being, and the purpose behind our mission.

As such, my philosophy has always been *bend it but never break it*.

To bend the rules is not to disregard them but to understand them and apply them with discernment when necessary. It means recognizing when conventional approaches are no longer serving us. Foster a mindset where the status quo must sometimes be challenged to progress and stay relevant. To bend the rules is to understand them deeply and to see the spaces between the lines where there's room for improvement and innovation. To bend the rules means to see past the overly used mentality of "but we've always done it this way" or letting complacency settle in as the norm.

NOTE   Bending the rules sometimes means having to risk popularity for progress without breaking your spirit and compromising your well-being.

So, bend the rules, but use common sense and intuition to avoid breaking anything that is irreversible. Your determination should never come at the cost of your health, the company's health, your family's well-being, or your teammates' spirit. How then can one inspire change, foster resilience, stay relevant, and remain obsessively goal-oriented without compromising the health and well-being of yourself, the company, and everyone around you?

The Framework

Outlined in this chapter is a framework I use that encapsulates five key principles that will help you create change without the cost of breaking the bank, breaking the spirit, and breaking your business:

1. Ask "why?"

2. Develop your AI strategy.

3. Think big, start small, scale quickly.

4. Choose your technology partner.

5. Pace yourself.

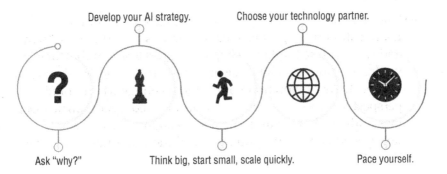

Develop your AI strategy.   Choose your technology partner.

Ask "why?"   Think big, start small, scale quickly.   Pace yourself.

Ask "Why?"

Technology is never the solution but a means to achieving a business or personal goal. Before you start anything, ask yourself, "Why do I need to do this?" It could be for the simple reason that you need to streamline your business operations so you can increase your earnings before interest, taxes, depreciation, and amortization (EBIDA) to 40% to sell your business to a private equity firm in two years and happily retire. That's totally acceptable. It could also be because competition is getting tough, and you need to stand out from the crowd.

Whatever your reasons may be, the goal is to drive business value, minimize friction, and know why you're doing it. This may sound obvious, but in my 20+ years of deployment experience I have witnessed numerous instances where leaders and project teams have overlooked this crucial step of openly discussing the "why" (the operative word being *openly*). I've noticed this happens for a few reasons:

- A lot of people like to focus on the shiny new object. Talking about the cool new tool is always more exciting than talking about the problem itself, so the "why" gets skipped.

- Leaders assume people know the business value; it's obvious to them, so it must be obvious to all. Therefore, it gets skipped, or the communication is insufficient.

This oversight leads to projects being initiated without a clear understanding of the ultimate objective, leading to chaos, confusion, and fragmented focus mid-journey.

So, as the rogue leader spearheading this undertaking:

- Your first objective is to reflect and ask yourself the "why." Make sure you have a good reason for doing this; otherwise, don't move forward!

- Once you have a "why," proactively engage with your leadership team, cofounders, partners, or teammates. Discuss your "why" and what you're thinking. Help them get a grasp of the direction you're heading, all while assisting them in discovering their own unique "why." If you find yourself in meetings where conflicting perspectives are shared, don't hesitate to schedule additional meetings until you have some semblance of alignment. Remember, you don't need consensus; you just need them to understand your "why."

Again, I know this all sounds obvious, and maybe I'm stating the obvious, but with tech projects, especially with AI projects, it's perhaps the number-one thing I've witness get skipped because everyone wants to jump straight into solutioning and the "cool" tool without reflecting on the "why" you're starting this project.

Develop Your AI Strategy

This is perhaps my favorite part of the project. It requires critical thinking, brainstorming, and group thinking. It's an exercise that brings people together and stretches our human capacity to think beyond what we know today.

After having done more strategy, brainstorming, and ideation sessions than I can count, I've learned not everyone is cut out for this type of exercise; be careful with who you invite to the sessions (more on that in Chapter 5 when we discuss your project killers).

While I won't go into detail in this chapter—we'll discuss the "what" and "how" in Chapter 4—I will cover the basics of an AI strategy here.

Building an enterprise-grade, highly reliant, and stable AI capability within an enterprise requires expertise, lots of funding, or both. I'm often brought in to develop a three-to-five-year roadmap that helps businesses develop a vision with objectives and capabilities outlined, key performance indicators (KPIs) established, and infrastructure, data, talent, engineering, development, change management and business needs highlighted.

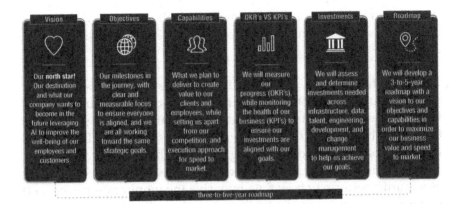

Vision	Objectives	Capabilities	OKR's VS KPI's	Investments	Roadmap
Our **north star!** Our destination and what our company wants to become in the future leveraging AI to improve the well-being of our employees and customers.	Our milestones in the journey, with clear and measurable focus to ensure everyone is aligned, and we are all working toward the same strategic goals.	What we plan to deliver to create value to our clients and employees, while setting us apart from our competition, and execution approach for speed to market.	We will measure our progress (OKR's), while monitoring the health of our business (KPI's) to ensure our investments are aligned with our goals.	We will assess and determine investments needed across infrastructure, data, talent, engineering, development, and change management to help us achieve our goals.	We will develop a 3-to-5-year roadmap with a vision to our objectives and capabilities in order to maximize our business value and speed to market.

three-to-five-year roadmap

To be clear, that's not what I'm asking you to do. What we're doing here is much simpler and focused on deploying a successful AI project based on your current capabilities and maturity. To do this, you want to figure out which of these five strategies you want to aim for:

The Efficiency Strategy   Efficiency is making sure you do the right things with minimal waste of time, resources, and effort. For AI deployments, this strategy is the least complex of them all. It requires minimal to no data and minimal to no defined business processes, and your workforce can be generalists, meaning you don't need a specialist to deploy the AI capabilities to experience business outcomes.

The Effectiveness Strategy   Effectiveness is making sure you do the right things to achieve the desired result or outcome. It's making sure the task is accomplished perfectly without necessarily being time-bound. For AI deployments, this strategy is not complex but will require more thinking, more time, minimal to no data, and some defined business processes.

The Productivity Strategy   Productivity is making sure you do the most you can with what you're given. It's about maximizing your output in a specific time frame and having a higher tolerance for inaccuracies. For AI deployments, this strategy is not complex but your selection of use case is key as it will determine if you need both good and accessible data, along with well-defined business processes.

The Expert Strategy   This area is focused on having deep domain knowledge and/or expertise in a certain area. It relies on proven methodologies and best practices and is geared toward solving problems. For AI deployments, this strategy is the most complex with minimal to no room for error. The reason it's the most difficult is because it requires a technical team, a lot of good clean data, well-defined business processes, and focus.

The Growth Strategy   This area is focused on external growth, usually achieved through customer acquisition, market share capture, impressions on your website, traffic on social media, and more. It's externally facing, so whatever you develop leaves an impression on the Internet and requires monitoring and measuring to ensure the growth you hoped is achieved with no negative consequences. It does require a certain level of maturity because of how data intensive the monitoring can be, and you need specialists who know their domain well to track progress.

In Chapter 4, we'll discuss how to select the strategy best suited for you. For now, just know selecting a strategy is key because it gives you a concrete and solid place to start that's grounded in reality. It helps you narrow down the use cases to the relevant ones. It gives you a focused path, gives your team a direction, and considers the reality of your environment and what you can reasonably take on.

NOTE   It's important to note that not any one of the five strategies is more or less important than the other. It's all about what's important to you and what you can realistically deploy, successfully, based on your company's current maturity.

While our goal is to be innovative, relevant, competitive, and forward looking, our approach is to bend it but not break it, so be smart in how you approach your AI project by starting with a strategy that you can realistically deploy.

Think Big, Start Small, Scale Quickly

I've been saying "Let's think big, start small, and then scale quickly" for nearly a decade. I learned this principle first at IBM when I was helping clients brainstorm how to best leverage AI within their operations. I quickly learned executives and stakeholders knew how to think big, but they also wanted to start big, not thinking through the risk implications.

I had this one client who was a large commercial bank, and they wanted to put in automated tellers to reduce their workforce within their teller division and reallocate the resources to another growing division. Sounded great. However, their clientele was mostly veterans and those in retirement. Well. . .while I don't mean to be agist, I would guess that individuals older than 65 are not the best demographic for testing new computer-based automated tellers. That demographic still prefers in-person human interactions. Needless to say, I talked them out of it, and we approached things that were more reasonable.

The three areas to consider include:

Thinking Big   This is all about the art of the possible: embracing the opportunities and imagining the possibilities. It's envisioning the possibilities for both your business and your personal life and uncovering ways to enhance them by reclaiming valuable time, maximizing savings, and channeling energy toward tasks and activities that give back. We don't let restraints, resources, and funding hold us back. We just think about the possibilities.

Starting Small   Imagine you're a budding gardener testing your green thumb. Would you start with landscaping and planting an entire garden or nurturing a small spot first? This strategy is all about being realistic with what's feasible and considering the practicalities of your business landscape to minimize risks, avoid squandering money, and save precious time. It's like flexing your muscles in preparation for a more significant challenge! By starting small, a use case that suits your organizational maturity and resources, you gain first hand experience with the processes, learn valuable lessons, and set yourself up for success on a grander scale.

Scaling Quickly   In the pursuit of innovation, thinking big is about laying the foundation of bigger things, starting small is about mitigating risk by biting off what you can chew, and scaling quickly is about commitment. When transitioning to scaling, avoid analysis paralysis at all costs. As leaders, being decisive is paramount. After you've evaluated the output, looked at the data, and measured the business benefits, make the decision to either productionize your proof of concept (POC) into full-scale production or pivot toward a new use case. This time period is critical as it signals your intentions to your team. Our objective is to avoid decisional stagnation in pursuit of rapid and informed actions.

Choose Your Technology Partner

It's safe to say you're not an AI expert. If I'm being totally honest, at this pace of change, no one is; a even "experts" are struggling to keep up. However, you're probably not as well-versed in the intricacies of artificial intelligence as someone who has been in the space, so partner up. An AI expert will serve as a consultant for you and your leadership team but also as a catalyst that maintains the drive and clarity your team is going to need with this critical initiative. Who you choose to partner with will set realistic expectations, offer reassurance, and constructively align your AI initiatives with your business vision, keeping everyone accountable for their part in the action and innovation you're driving.

With that in mind, not all experts are created equal. You have technical individuals who are super smart but can sometimes over-complicate things, be abrasive, or, worse, culturally create unnecessary tension. You have high-level functional consultants who are great at getting alignment, get along with your team, but are too high level and can only provide best practices. You ultimately have to assess what's right for you.

I'm personally a techno-functional expert. I can swing left and geek out with your data and engineering teams about feature extraction and semantic layers all day. I can also swing right and speak with your leadership team and board of directors about the business benefits with clear OKRs and KPIs outlined. We come in all shapes and sizes! Find what's best for you and your organization.

If you're starting out, I suggest a few guiding principles:

- I do not recommend starting with a big management consulting firm (unless you're a Fortune 500) because big firms don't do small projects with small budgets. Pick a boutique firm that is right-sized for your budget and ambitions.

- The market is saturated with AI advisors, AI strategists, and AI development firms. Interview a few and pick the team that aligns with your culture the most, is hungry to do great work, has a strong development team, and has a leader who won't bait and switch. They will be with you through the end. The cultural fit is important because your team will need to work with someone they trust.

- If the answer isn't a hard yes, then it's a hard no. Validate their qualifications, but also trust your gut and intuition. If it doesn't feel right, don't partner with them, plain and simple. You can't measure feelings, intuition, and experience, yet they are important forces. While impossible to measure, decide if they are the right mindset match for you and your project.

Pace Yourself

Change is hard. Really hard. If it was easy, it would have been done by now. Why? With it come commitments that many aren't willing to put in; we hear about the CEOs, founders, and Silicon Valley entrepreneurs working 100–120 a week for several years, nearly killing themselves with exhaustion. We don't need to be that when deploying AI. While this is new territory for you and you'll be learning on the job, pace yourself. Balance your drive for innovation and change with the realities of your organization's maturity and culture. By that I mean measure the pace at which the company naturally moves and sets realistic expectations for how long something will take, and then manage your energy accordingly. I can't tell you how important this is to avoid burnout and keep your energy up for the long haul.

I'll tell you a little personal story since I learned this the hard way.

About a year ago I was diagnosed with having chronic fatigue because I had triggered a dormant Epstein-Barr virus (EBV) that put me down for several months. Nearly 95% of Americans have the virus, but it remains dormant until a trigger causes it to activate. The diagnosis was that my adrenal glands were cooked; I went too hard, too long, and too fast, and it activated the virus. My body was done, and therefore it decided to shut down every day like clockwork. The worst part was, when I first started experiencing the tiredness, I didn't think anything of it. I just pushed through with caffeine and grit, which made it worse.

What I felt was intense fatigue; it wasn't my usual "transformation program tiredness." It felt far more intense, and it was a daily occurrence that seemed to be timed with the precision of a Swiss watch. It was as though my body had made a pact with the clock, agreeing to succumb to exhaustion every day at exactly 1:30 p.m.

This was more than just an inconvenience. It was a debilitating tiredness that made it difficult for me to keep up with my work schedule. My afternoons were typically filled with Zoom calls, and I found myself struggling to stay alert and focused. Concentrating on the meetings became an uphill battle, one that I often felt I was losing.

There were days when I could barely make it through the virtual calls. I would stare at my screen with my thoughts a million miles away. On some days I had no choice but to cancel the calls. On others, I was forced to delegate them to my team, hoping they would understand. It wasn't just the physical toll that was concerning; it was also the change in my behavior and my demeanor that began to worry me. I started noticing that when I did manage to show up for these calls, I was not the same person. I was cranky and irritable, and people could see the exhaustion in my eyes.

These are traits one cannot afford to exhibit, especially when you are in a position effecting change. In such a role, you need to inspire confidence and trust, not doubt and discomfort. I knew that if I didn't find a way to manage my fatigue, I risked losing the respect and support of those around me and all that I had worked for. As a result, I took some time off, worked on my health, got it back to a relatively stable state, and changed my approach in all my transformations through what I call the *multiplier effect*.

How does the multiplier effect work, and why does it help in pacing yourself? The calculation is simple really. Here's what you need to do:

1. Estimate the timeline of your project.
2. Understand the culture and pace of your organization.
3. Understand your own personal pace.
4. Apply the formula I've provided.

For starters, estimating your project doesn't need to be perfect.

- Go through your normal estimation processes and then add 30%. The 30% is your learning curve multiplier for AI. As an example, if you estimate your AI project to take three months, make your new estimates four months (3 * 1.3 = 4 month).

- Next, take your new estimates of four months, and add your corporate culture multiplier, which ranges from 25% to 100%, with 25% designated for organizations and teams that are fast, agile, decisive, and adapt quickly to innovation. If your company is slower in nature, deliberate, and political, your multiplier would be 100%. As an example, let's take a company that is conservative. They take their time and tend to have long alignment discussions. However, the company is very top-down oriented, so once a decision is made among stakeholders, the company aligns and moves fast. I would give this company a multiplier of 50%. As such, our four months will now increase to six months (4 * 1.5 = 6 months).

- Next, measure your personal pace and add a multiplier of –30% to 50% to your current projections. Your ability to influence, push, and keep the momentum of the project is highly dependent on you as the leader and your natural pace and tenacity. So, if you're easygoing, conservative, and don't push, add 50% on top of your estimates. If, however, you move fast and are bullish with your approach (like me), reduce your estimates by –30% because you're likely going to be impatient with progress and will nudge the team to move faster. As an example, let's say your style is somewhere in the middle: take your six months and add the amplifier of 10%

(10% being the middle of –30% and 50%). Your new estimates will be 6.5 months.

As a summary, what you originally estimated to be four months is now 6.5 months. While at first glance this change may seem like a setback, it provides an unexpected advantage. The revised project estimates now allow us the luxury of a more measured approach. We can plan our tasks more strategically, considering not just the urgency of the tasks but also the physical and mental energy levels of everyone, including yourself. Instead of pushing ourselves to the brink of exhaustion in a relentless pursuit of an unrealistically tight deadline, where we can skip steps needed in preparation and rush through decisions, we can now approach our work in a more balanced and sustainable way, while respecting our limits in the process.

In my experience, I've learned this helps increase the probability of success with new AI deployments, and it helps rally the people around you, leaving an impression of "Well, that wasn't so bad!"

NOTE   A word of caution. . .when you add the multiplier effect across the learning curve, company culture, and your natural cadence, it's likely you'll come up with estimates two to three times more than you had expected. From an approach perspective, that's fine. What you have to maniacally watch for is keeping the excitement, energy levels, and focus of the team intact while you extend the timeline. It's one thing to keep people engaged for four months; it's another to keep them energetic and motived for 6.5 months, especially with all the competing priorities. Make sure to carve out time to celebrate small victories and keep the energy going.

The Five Pillars

As we close this chapter, keep in mind that bending the rules is a strategic endeavor, not an act of rebellion.

It's a deliberate process of examining and reinterpreting the norms that govern us to move beyond our comfort zone. However, striking a balance between ambition and well-being is paramount. As leaders, we must navigate change without compromising our well-being, our company's integrity, or the morale of our teams. The goal is to inspire change and build resilience while safeguarding the health and spirit of ourselves and those we lead.

The five foundational pillars in this chapter serve as your roadmap to implement transformational change responsibly.

1. Ask "why?"
2. Develop your AI strategy.
3. Think big, start small, scale quickly.
4. Choose your technology partner.
5. Pace yourself.

Follow these principles and you will lead not just with intelligence and ambition but with wisdom and compassion, ensuring that while you may bend the rules, you will never break the spirit.

How to Start

The goal of this chapter is to help you be successful with AI projects without having a technical background. Contrary to what most people believe, having a technical background is not necessary. While at some point you may need to bring in technical resources, it's a sliver in time compared to the entire project. The success of your AI project has to do with three things: preparation, people, and perseverance. In this chapter, we go through all three without theoretical nonsense.

We'll discuss a six-phase operational framework; after introducing each phase, we'll discuss how to exactly approach each of the six phases and what needs to be done in each phase.

This chapter, unlike the others, is instructional in nature. It's important for you to note the following:

- The extent of work you need to do within each step of the framework will depend on you and your company culture. By this I mean the level of discussions, decisions, and documentation will vary, so don't get overwhelmed. For example, when deciding which of the five AI strategies is right for you, this may take you several months or half a day. Regardless, I've outlined all five strategies and the readiness assessment to help you select the right one, but how long each step will take depends on your influence and environment.

■ Additionally, this chapter is an intensive step-by-step guide. You'll see a lot more flowchart, diagrams, bullet points, sequencing of activities, and more. There's less narration and more step-by-step instructions on how to select a strategy; select your use case; and prepare, design, solve, and deploy your AI project. It's much more detailed and focused on outlining the steps, the activities, and the questions, and I will walk you through how to put it all together.

Let's begin!

The Experience You Need

In a 2023 poll conducted by Boston Consulting Group (BCG) of more than 1,400 C-suite executives, 66% said they were ambivalent about or outright dissatisfied with their organization's progress on generative AI. Respondents cited a shortage of talent, unclear roadmaps, and an absence of strategy around deploying generative AI responsibly. Yet, 89% said that generative AI still ranked as their "top three" technology initiatives for their companies in 2024.

Let's take another look, this time from Harvard Business Review and Investopedia in 2023. A majority of CEOs, executives, and C-suite officers have little faith in their organization's expertise in implementing AI, are concerned about data, and/or don't feel comfortable using the insights coming from their analytical systems.

does not believe "their organization **has the expertise** to implement AI."

have "concerns about **data security** [and] the technology's **bias and accuracy.**"

"say they are '**not comfortable**' assessing or using data from advanced analytics systems."

These are grim findings unfortunately.

Frankly, I'm not surprised. Only a handful of people in the world have experience with deploying AI projects at scale for businesses, and I'm talking about real, practical, scraped knees and bruised elbow experiences that are relevant for you. Lucky for you, I happen to be one of them. I come from delivery experience, and I will share with you frameworks, toolkits, questionnaires, strategies, and the dos and don'ts of deploying AI so that you don't become one these disgruntled leaders.

First, let's address the major theme of "not having experience" as the primary factor in not moving forward with AI-based projects. Remember, you won't know it until you try it. That's true with everything in life, so not having experience is a silly reason not to try something.

Also, the reality of not having "experience" isn't a monolithic concept. It's a multidimensional concept, and the reasons why AI projects don't succeed is not because of "experience" per se; it's because AI projects fall victim to one of these five problems:

- Companies don't know how to start, so they don't start. They let lack of inertia get in their way.

- Companies start but can't get consensus on where to go and how to start, so analysis paralysis stops them from landing on a deployable use case.

- Companies have too many competing strategic priorities, so they can't get the focus, funding, and necessary facilitation to get organizational alignment and buy-in.

- Companies start a proof of concept but without the right resources, guidance, and expertise from experts. Something that should take two to five months takes six to nine months. As a result, they lose the attention span of leadership and support dissipates.

- Companies complete the POC and realize the business value, but they don't know how to scale and operationalize the capability because of the organizational hurdles that come with workforce change management and maintenance.

The experience you need comes from knowing how to overcome and bypass these reasons, and I will walk you through the how. We'll start with the basics and then build up. For example, a typical deployment approach tends to follow a 5, 10, 20, 30, 20, 10, 5 model:

TIME COMMITMENT	ACTIVITY
5%	Inertia to start
10%	Picking your team
20%	Strategy and use case
30%	Design and solutioning
20%	Deployment
10%	Iterations
5%	Go/no-go

Let's break this down.

- 5% is dedicated to getting over the inertia to start and not analyze it too much.
- 10% of your time will be dedicated to finding the right team. The right teammates have grit, ambition, and resilience. They have an inner rogue in them too, and they are mostly non-technical resources. We'll discuss that in greater detail in Chapter 5.
- 20% is dedicated to strategy and use-case selection.
- 30% dedicated to preparation, designing, and solutioning.
- 20% dedicated to deployment. This is where some technical expertise could help, but you can deploy AI without a technical expert if you choose an off-the-shelf solution.
- 10% is dedicated to reviews and iterations.
- 5% dedicated to the go/no-go decision to scale.

While AI may seem like a technical concept and some solutions can be very technical and complex in nature, you'll learn other ways of deploying AI that don't require you to have someone with a PhD on your team. Thanks to the current advancements of AI, the market is flooded with off-the-shelf and off-the-model solutions (we'll get to those shortly), and with those solutions, you'll learn your AI deployment has little to do with the technicalities and tool itself and more to do with picking the right strategy, the right use case, the right team, and the planning and preparation that goes before solutioning.

Framework for AI Initiatives

The six-phase framework we're going to go through will help you with these success factors and include:

1. Conducting an AI readiness assessment
2. Selecting an AI strategy
3. Creating and selecting use cases
4. Preparing and designing
5. Creating solutions
6. Deploying and going live

Before we get into the weeds, there are two things to note. First, the six-phase framework is a step-by-step guide for you and your team. It will walk you through activities, give you decision points, and provide strategies and guardrails for what needs to be discussed and decided so you can have a successful deployment.

- Phases 1 and 6 are light in content and mostly based on common sense (which isn't so common unfortunately)
- Phase 2 gets a little richer with content.
- Phases 3, 4, and 5 are the heaviest in nature. Make sure you're caffeinated and in a distraction-free zone.

I just want to set those expectations up front so you know what lies ahead. Second, the extent of work you need to do for each phase is dependent on your style and your company's culture. Here's what I mean:

Personal Style   We're not all created equal. Some of us are big-picture folks, while others live in the details. You decide if you want to delegate the preparation and documentation for each phase to someone else more detailed or keep it for yourself. In either case, you can't skip the steps. They must all be covered, discussed, and documented, and if you're the one reading this book, you must be involved.

Company Culture   If you're the CEO of a 10-person digital marketing agency, the likeliness is that the level of detail you're going to get into across the six phases will be light. You'll have fewer meetings and fewer documents, and the level of depth and conversation will be narrow since decision-making rights will be fairly centralized to a few folks. You don't need to get overwhelmed with the steps outlined in this chapter; just go through them. If, however, you're a business leader running a manufacturing company with nearly 1,000 employees and you're SOX compliant and Six Sigma certified, you're going to go into a lot of detail with the documentation, decision-making rights, protocols, workflows, governance, etc.

As such, one size does not fit all. The key is to go through all six phases, follow the steps, have the discussions, and make the decisions with the right people in the room. The level of depth you go into, the speed at which you make the decisions, and the level of documentation are completely dependent on your style and company culture. Since I'm biased for action, let's get into it! The following shows the six-phase AI deployment framework:

1	2	3	4	5	6
Readiness Assessment	**Selecting Your AI Strategy**	**Use Case Ideation & Selection**	**Preparation & Designing**	**Solutioning**	**Implementation & Go-Live**
This will be a quick gut-check as to how ready you and your organization are to deploy AI. It's not meant to stop you from preceding, but meant to tell you where you'll likely succeed with your current maturity and capabilities.	Your AI strategy will serve as a compass for your use case ideation session, business objectives, & outcomes. It's a great way to keep the discussions focused.	This phase has two components ideating your use case to align with your strategy, and selecting a use case that not only delivers value, but your organization has the ability to deliver.	This step will help you create a blueprint that will outline your budget, resources, activities, tasks, and workflows. You choose the partnerships and technical expertise you need.	The solution phase is about how you turn your designs into reality. This is where you research your AI tools and partner with the technical expertise you need.	This is where you take your preparation and begin implementing. You will spin it up, iterate, and validate if the outcomes pass your go/no-go criteria.

Phase 1: Conducting a readiness assessment: This will be a quick, gut-check assessment as to how ready you are for AI and where you should focus your attention. It's not meant to stop you from preceding by any means. The goal is to help you select an AI strategy aligned with your current maturity and capabilities, while also making you have enough focus and sponsorship to get it done.

Phase 2: Selecting an AI strategy: Your AI strategy will help you develop a compass for your use cases, which will drive your desired business outcomes. The goal of this phase is to pick an AI strategy aligned with your maturity and your business goals and to avoid scope creep and any potential risks that pull you away from your core purpose.

Phase 3: Creating and selecting use cases: Use case ideation and selection should align with your AI strategy. The goal is to stay focused and help avoid free-form, unstructured ideation sessions. The free-form approach can waste time and be infective for larger organizations that are more consensus based. You will hit stalemate very quickly and create "alignment drag." Our objective with this phase will be to ideate use cases relevant for your strategy only and select use cases based on a methodology I will introduce ("Complexity vs. Criticality").

Phase 4: Preparing and designing: The design phase of this six-phase development framework is a critical stage where you and your team will develop and outline the specifics of your AI project, based on the AI use case you chose and the "AI Essentials" playbook I will provide. The objective will be to discuss, decide, and document your blueprint using the playbook.

Phase 5: Selecting a solution: The solutioning phase for AI projects is not embedded in the design phase. This is a key mistake folks make. Design is about what the end AI capability should look like, whereas the solutioning phase is about how you turn those designs into reality. Too many people jumble and combine the conversations into one; please don't. Keep them separate with a clear division of labor. The three outcomes in this phase are to research your off-the-shelf AI solutions, select your solution, and establish your deployment plan.

Phase 6: Deploying and going live: This is where you select your solution, register, activate, experiment, iterate, create your standard operating procedures (SOPs), and deploy your solution.

We will discuss the decision of "buy versus build" in phases 5 and 6; the decision-making process is fairly straightforward. As a business leader, owner, or practitioner, I suggest you never build from scratch and instead leverage the countless off-the-shelf solutions. Loads of wonderful AI-based companies have solved complex problems already. Leverage the shoulder (and expertise) of giants and accelerate your journey by buying software or a tool that enables speed to market.

Phase 1: Conducting a Readiness Assessment

The goal of phase 1 is to ask a few questions and get an understanding of where you are as a company and as a team to help steer you in the right path with strategy, use cases, and culture considerations in your approach.

**Readiness
Assessment**

This will be a quick gut-check as to how ready you and your organization are to deploy AI. It's not meant to stop you from preceding, but meant to tell you where you'll likely succeed with your current maturity and capabilities.

- **6 Categories**
- **12 Questions**
- **Identify Your AI Strategy**

The questions are simple by design and straightforward in determining where you need to focus your AI efforts to help you establish a strategy. The questions are grouped into six (6) categories.

- Market strategy
- Business understanding
- Workforce acumen
- Company culture
- Role of technology
- Data

Each of the six categories has two questions. After you answer each question, there will be a grading score at the end. The scores will help you align with an AI strategy.

As a reminder, you're always welcome to spend $200–$500,000 on an AI strategy and/or use-case identification with a management consulting firm. As a senior manager, I charged $400/hour, and as a partner I charged upward of $950/hour. I'm not saying don't do that if your CEO requires it, as sometimes larger companies do. What I am saying is, even if you leverage outside help, I recommend reading this book and becoming familiar with the six phases so you know what questions to ask and you don't blindly follow their framework and process.

NOTE   Outsourcing is a big decision to be made for companies. If it's a priority and you don't have the resources, then outsourcing could be your best bet. Regardless of your decision, come prepared with some knowledge.

If, however, hiring a management consulting firm is not in your wheelhouse, this chapter will be your bedrock, and phase 1 will be important for you.

Here's how the questionnaire works: You're going to see all six categories outlined. Read each of the questions (a and b) within the categories and answer each question, giving it a rating of 1 through 5. Then add up your total by category (with a minimum score of 2 and a maximum score of 10). Depending on where you fall within the 2–10 range, I've outlined an ideal strategy for you. Let's begin!

Readiness Questionnaire

1. Market Strategy

    a. We understand our business and market thoroughly and have rigorously identified, sized, and prioritized opportunities for growth.

Score

1	2	3	4	5
Light	**Emerging**	**Standard**	**Advanced**	**Thought Leaders**
Leadership may be aware of the priorities, but the company as a whole is unaware or has minimal knowledge.	We are starting to have focused discussions across the teams to get better aligned as a company.	Priorities have been identified, and some form of communication has occurred across the company.	The company and teams are in lockstep and clear KPIs and OKRs have been identified to align with the company's priorities.	The company is aligned, and we are leading the marketplace with both innovation and growth, setting industry standards.

b. We have a comprehensive view of our competitive landscape and have rigorously identified current and potential sources of new competition or disruption.

Score

1	2	3	4	5
Light	**Emerging**	**Standard**	**Advanced**	**Thought Leaders**
We are aware of our core competitors but tend to stay heads down and focused on our own growth.	We are aware of our core competitors and sometimes have discussions and perform a SWOT analysis.	We are aware of our competitors but can be in the dark with new incumbents. We tend to be reactive versus proactive.	We hire great talent and monitor the competitive landscape rigorously to know our market position and posture.	We have high-performing teams; we lead the industry and create the competition for our industry.

2. Business Understanding

a. We have clarity on existing business problems and are actively addressing them through a variety of projects and programs because we believe in continuous improvement.

Score

1	2	3	4	5
Light	**Emerging**	**Standard**	**Advanced**	**Thought Leaders**
We have tons of business problems but live with them because we're too focused on our clients.	We have identified our business problems but usually don't take immediate action.	We have prioritized the problems and identified the solutions, but focus and funding are our challenges.	We have put together a roadmap for our fixes and are actively working on projects this year.	The company is very focused on continuous improvement and actively engages In yearly projects.

b. We have clear business processes with roles, accountability, documentation, and workflows aligned for all teams and functions to follow.

Score

1	2	3	4	5
Light	**Emerging**	**Standard**	**Advanced**	**Thought Leaders**
We really don't have formal processes or documentation in place; people get things done.	We have some processes in place with some documentation but rely mostly on people.	Most teams have some processes and documentation in place, and we try to follow them.	Most teams have some processes, documentation, and workflows, and they are well communicated.	We are hyper-focused on efficiency; processes and documents are followed.

3. Workforce Acumen

    a. We have a workforce of strong business acumen, domain expertise, and specialization within our organization.

Score

1	2	3	4	5
Light	**Emerging**	**Standard**	**Advanced**	**Thought Leaders**
Our talent base is comprised of mostly generalists, and we figure things out as we go along.	We are mostly generalists but have started hiring specialists in key areas of the company.	We are a mix of generalists and specialists and know who to go to when we have questions.	We are mostly comprised of specialists by function and domain, and have clear roles and responsibilities.	We are specialists who operate as strategic thinkers while also hands-on with the details.

b. We have a team that is always willing and able, and values opportunity versus consequence and risk.

Score

1	2	3	4	5
Light	Emerging	Standard	Advanced	Thought Leaders
Risk exposure is the first thing we assess before looking at the merits of any project or engagement.	We assess both risk and possibilities. We are very selective with the types of projects we take on.	We are mostly willing and able; however, our day jobs keep us busy, so it's a matter of time not risk.	We strike a balance and make room for opportunity-based projects while proactively mitigating risk.	We hire innovators, early adopters, and those with a growth mindset so we can continuously innovate.

4. Company Culture

   a. Our company is centered around taking on new and innovative projects. We are always evolving and adapting; it's an expectation for our workforce.

Score

1	2	3	4	5
Light	Emerging	Standard	Advanced	Thought Leaders
Although we have good intentions, we tend to do things the same way year after year.	We've started engaging in more business improvement discussions and activities, albeit slowly.	We've begun experimenting and are actively testing new concepts across functions.	Our portfolio of projects is a mix, and innovation always plays a strong role in the mix.	We have a dedicated team and an innovation lab to test and try the latest advancements.

b. Leadership mandates goals for teams to drive greater efficiency, effectiveness, and productivity as a means to scale.

Score

1	2	3	4	5
Light	**Emerging**	**Standard**	**Advanced**	**Thought Leaders**
Leadership isn't focused on innovation or new tech. We're mostly a company of operators.	We stick with the basics but discuss possibilities. Leadership supports selective projects.	We run the business with what we know, but leadership often asks us to look at new things frequently.	Leadership mandates we look at ways to improve efficiency, effectiveness, and productivity.	We have top-down mandates that carry over into our yearly performance reviews.

5. Role of Technology

a. Technology is a major enabler for our strategic priorities; we have several projects in flight.

Score

1	2	3	4	5
Light	**Emerging**	**Standard**	**Advanced**	**Thought Leaders**
We're not a company that's dependent on tech except for email, Excel, Word, and PowerPoint.	We are starting to explore tech for sales, marketing, client relations, operations, and more.	While we are not tech-centric per se, all of our processes have a dependency on tech.	We are heavily invested in upgrades and modernizing our tech stack; we have several projects in flight.	We are a company that has tech at its core, and our capabilities and team are advanced.

b. We have a technology team that's reliable and knowledgeable. They are our partners in everything we do and bring forward ideas where technology can help.

Score

1	2	3	4	5
Light	Emerging	Standard	Advanced	Thought Leaders
We have one person who manages everything, and they handle all the requests from the company.	We have a single point of contact, and a few contractors we depend on for anything tech-related.	We have a team that manages the systems we use; we rely on them for uptime.	We have a mature team that manages all the systems. We rely on them heavily for all deployments.	We have a mature team that operate as our partners, and they attend all discussions.

6. Data

a. The data you think you may need is accessible and available for use.

Score

1	2	3	4	5
Light	Emerging	Standard	Advanced	Thought Leaders
I'm not sure what data we need honestly, nor do I know who to ask for it.	We have data; I know who to ask for it, but I'm not sure if it's what we need.	I know where the data resides and who can help me with any data needs.	I know where the data resides; I have access to it whenever I need it.	We have strong self-service practices; our data is accessible and analyzed.

b. The data you think you may need is clean and of good quality for AI use.

Score

1	2	3	4	5
Light	**Emerging**	**Standard**	**Advanced**	**Thought Leaders**
I honestly don't know and who to ask	I don't know but I know who to ask	I think its good, but I know who to ask to verify	Some areas are good and others are bad, it really depends	Our data is of good quality and we can depend on it

Questionnaire Results

Your score on the assessment will serve as an aid in determining your AI strategy. While useful, it's important to remember this is still only a guide and to be used for consideration. You may want to further investigate or validate your findings with your team.

Here's how to assess your score: Go through each of the six categories and the two questions (a and b) in each, and write down your score of 1 through 5. Add up your scores for each category. The minimum score for each subsection is 2 (1+1), and the maximum is 10 (5+5). Once you have a score, look at the following scoring matrix. This will help you define which AI strategies and approaches are best suited for you and your team considering your current capabilities and maturity. To recap, there are five AI strategies, as we discussed in Chapter 3. We'll go through each in detail in phase 2. For now, just write down the recommendations.

Market Strategy: This section is all about knowing your business well enough to know it's not just about avoiding competitor or industry threats but about outpacing the industry norm and giving yourself a strategic advantage. Adopting AI is viewed as defensive posturing but right now is a great window to make it an offensive one. The score in this section indicates how well you and your team have macro knowledge of your industry and its immanent threats.

MARKET STRATEGY SUBTOTAL	DESCRIPTION
2–4	The knowledge seems to be centralized within the leadership team only, and not the company. As such, you're going to have a hard time with anything "growth-based," "expert-based," or "effectivity-based" since these strategies require strong and deep knowledge across your organization. The advice is to focus your AI strategy on "efficiency" and/or "productivity-based" AI projects.
5–7	There seems to be broader knowledge on market opportunities and threats; it's not just contained within a small circle or the leadership team. As such, you can focus on "efficiency-based," "productivity-based," or "effectiveness-based" AI strategies.
8–10	All five strategies are available to you because you and your team have a strong sense of the business landscape and you're aligned on internal priorities.

Business Understanding: This section is all about having clarity on your business problems and processes. The information should be common knowledge, and the team should have an active interest in addressing business priorities and putting in place mechanisms to ensure smooth operations.

BUSINESS UNDERSTANDING SUBTOTAL	DESCRIPTION
2–4	There are a lot of inefficiencies within your organization and you're not prioritizing the fixes. The suggestion would be to focus on an "efficiency-based" strategy as it's the easiest to deploy. All other strategies require some level of defined business processes, but you and your company aren't there yet.
5–7	You can expand your reach into "efficiency-based," "productivity-based," or "effectiveness-based" AI strategies.

BUSINESS UNDERSTANDING SUBTOTAL	DESCRIPTION
8–10	All five strategies are available to you because you and your team have a strong sense of the business problems and processes, you're proactively addressing them and have internal alignment. Therefore "growth-based" and "expert-based" strategies won't be too much of a stretch for you.

Workforce Acumen: This section is about understanding your workforce and how deep into the details they can go within a given domain or subject area, while also having the growth-based mindset to explore and try new things (versus accepting status quo).

WORKFORCE ACUMEN SUBTOTAL	DESCRIPTION
2–4	Working with your existing team is going to be a challenge; you're going to have to supplement their institutional knowledge with specialty knowledge and some go-getter horsepower to see opportunity rather than risk. As such, when selecting your AI strategy, try to focus on "efficiency-based" projects to avoid over-stretching your team's abilities. Remember the goal is always to bend, but never to break.
5–7	You may be able to expand your reach and explore "efficiency-based," "productivity-based," or "effectiveness-based" AI strategies with the team you have.
8–10	All five strategies are available to you and your team because they have domain and subject-matter expertise and are used to taking on new projects that push and challenge the status quo. Therefore, "growth-based" and "expert-based" strategies won't be too much of a bend, and they could even thrive off the new stretch goals.

Company Culture: This section is about understanding your culture and seeing how focused you are on adapting and evolving to new capabilities due to pivoting cultural norms, leadership mandates, and the innovation mindset.

COMPANY CULTURE SUBTOTAL	DESCRIPTION
2–4	Your existing team will need to be supplemented with specialty knowledge and some go-getter horsepower no matter what AI strategy you choose. Start easy and go with the easiest type of strategy, an "efficiency-based" strategy to avoid over-stretching your team's abilities.
5–7	You may be able to expand your reach to "efficiency-based," "productivity-based," or "effectiveness-based" AI strategies with the team you have.
8–10	All five strategies are available to you and your team because you're used to adapting, pivoting, and evolving. Those traits are already engrained in the culture.

Role of Technology: This section is about understanding the role technology plays in your organization and the maturity of your team. While technology is not the primary marker for your AI success, it's good to understand where you are and how it can best align to your strategy.

ROLE OF TECHNOLOGY SUBTOTAL	DESCRIPTION
2–4	You're light on the tech side and mostly use standard office tools. I suggest keeping your first use case super simple and focus your AI strategy on "efficiency-based" and "productivity-based" strategies. The dependency on tech knowledge is a lot less with these two strategies.
5–7	You have enough of a foundation, so you can expand your strategy to include "effectiveness" and "growth-based" AI strategies.
8–10	All five strategies are available to you and your team.

Data: This section is about understanding if your data is accessible, available, and of good quality in case you need it for the use case you choose in your AI strategy.

DATA SUBTOTAL	DESCRIPTION
2–4	You're not sure of your data environment, so I advise sticking with use cases that have limited data dependency. This will largely focus your AI strategy on "efficiency-based" and "productivity-based" strategies.
5–7	You have a baseline knowledge of your data environment or at least know someone who does. While you're not totally novice in the arena, it's still advised to stay clear of use cases that have a high data dependency. This will limit your options to "efficiency-based" and "productivity-based" strategies.
8–10	All five strategies are available to you and your team.

After you've gone through each of the six sections, write down your dominant AI strategy. At the end of the next section, Phase 2, are some examples of how to blend this information into a decision.

Phase 2: Your AI Strategy

We've talked about the five strategies in phase 1, but we haven't gotten into any length or detail about what each strategy is and why picking one that is aligned to your organizational capabilities is key. In this chapter, we'll explore all five strategies and how they align with your existing organizational capabilities and maturity.

To start, your AI strategy is all about mapping your present state to a desired state, using AI as the accelerator in achieving that future state. This serves as a primer to help you and your organization stay focused while helping uncomplicate what may appear complicated. It will connect you to a purpose and align your organization, its current maturity, its mindset, and its momentum to act.

By selecting a strategy that's aligned with your purpose and organizational maturity (this last part is key), you have a great chance of succeeding. From here, you get to ideate use cases that allow you to solve a problem, leveraging AI.

Phase 2 is all about the strategy.

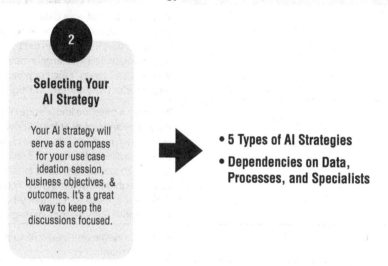

Let me re-introduce the five strategies and what they mean.

The Efficiency Strategy   Efficiency is making sure you do the right things with minimal waste of time, resources, and effort. For AI deployments, this strategy is the least complex of them all. You can deploy several use cases that are efficiency based with minimal to no data and minimal to no business processes defined, and your workforce can be full of generalists versus specialists. Meaning you don't need any specific or special type of talent to gain value and to experience business outcomes from AI. The use cases are also internally facing, which means it helps your team with little to no downside or risk exposure to clients because the use cases are not external facing. This is the safest route and option for any company attempting its first AI project.

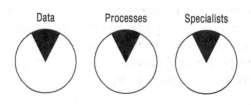

The Productivity Strategy Productivity is making sure you do the most you can with what you're given. It's about maximizing your output in a specific time frame but also having a higher tolerance for inaccuracies. The goal is really about getting things done as quickly as possible, without too many mistakes. This AI strategy is easy to deploy; however, depending on the use case you chose, you may need some data, and you may need some business processes defined. You can work with any workforce and be effective with a "productivity-based" strategy.

The Effectiveness Strategy Effectiveness is making sure you do the right things to achieve the desired result or outcome. It's making sure the task is accomplished perfectly without being time-bound. For AI deployments, this strategy is not complex but will require more thinking and time. It doesn't require data; however, business processes have to be defined, and you do need some specialists because the very nature of the job is about accuracy and results. The use cases are mostly internal, which means there's little to no downside or risk exposure to clients.

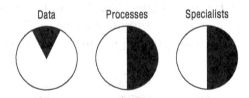

The Expert Strategy This area is focused on having deep domain knowledge and/or expertise in a certain area. It relies on proven methodologies and best practices and is geared toward solving problems. For AI deployments, this strategy is the most complex to deploy because it requires minimal to no error. It requires data, business processes, a specialized workforce, technical talent, and focus. Unless you're a mature organization, I would stay away from this AI strategy for now.

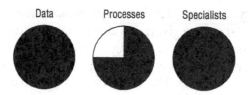

The Growth Strategy   The last of the five strategies is the "growth-based" strategy. I personally love this one, but it can get tricky with controls and protocols if you're not experienced. Why? This strategy is focused on growth which can be achieved in a variety of ways from growth in customer acquisition or growth in net promotor scores (NPSs). To do this, you may rely on customer service chat bots, content creation that drives traffic to your website, social media, and more. With growth-based strategies, most of the use cases are external-facing, so whatever you develop is likely to be seen in public. As such, it requires a level of accuracy suitable for the public, and monitoring and measuring controls to ensure the growth you hoped is achieved with no negative consequences to you and your potential customers. In Chapter 6, I go into detail about a "growth-based" strategy gone wrong. A simple mistake led to something atrocious. That's why this strategy requires a certain level of maturity because you're trying to put your best foot forward in public. It can also be data intensive, it requires analytical skills, and you need talent that has domain expertise to monitor both progress and public reactions. For this strategy, the risk exposure is higher. That's why I recommend starting off with an "efficiency-based," "productivity-based," or "effectiveness-based" strategy before taking on a "growth-based" strategy.

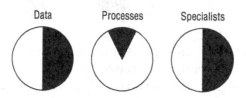

At this point, you may be wondering about the differences and intricacies of the five strategies. To illustrate the different strategies and how they play out, let's pick a simple analogy such as mowing a lawn. As you can tell, I like to uncomplicate the complicated.

Efficiency-based strategy: Your goal is to mow the lawn using the least amount of gas or electrical power. You'll probably want to plan an optimal route to reduce energy and waste. You'd like to create an even cut, but that's not your priority; saving time, cost, and resources is your priority.

Productivity-based strategy: Your goal is to mow the lawn as quickly as possible using anything within reach. You may miss patches and there could be some unevenness, but you're able to mow the lawn in half the time, and it's "good enough." You're able to get the job done and move onto the next task on your to-do list.

Effectiveness-based strategy: Your goal is to mow the perfect lawn. Your focus is on the quality of the job and not the cost or time it will take you to do it. You plan your day on how and when to cut the lawn. You'll even give some thought to landscaping and planting a flower patch with a garden chair to make it perfect. You want accuracy and perfection because those matter most with this particular strategy.

Expert-based strategy: Your goal is to mow the lawn flawlessly, and you analyze the type of mower, the size of the blade, the route path, and the weather patterns (and more) to ensure the ideal environment is created to cut the perfect lawn for you and your neighbors. You take pride in the intricate details that go into the planning and execution and so do your neighbors. They may even ask how you're able to get such a green and clean-cut lawn and you're more than happy to share your with them.

Growth-based strategy: While your goal was to focus on your own lawn, others noticed how well you took care of your lawn and asked you to take care of their lawn too. You decided to invest in a more powerful mower, bought more potent fertilizer, and hired staff. To pay off the investments, you need to simultaneously mow more lawns while attracting new customers and getting the word out there.

To review the flow of how all the pieces connect, Phase 1 is about understanding your maturity and guiding you to a plausible AI strategy. Phase 2 is about going deeper into each strategy and explaining what they are and the reasons for suitability. Phase 3, up next, is about ideation and selecting a use case that aligns with your strategy.

Demonstration of How It Works

The following table presents the results of three companies. Each leader answered the questions, summed the subtotal, and wrote down the dominant strategy that was suggested.

	COMPANY #1	COMPANY #2	COMPANY #3
Market Strategy	Efficiency and Productivity	All five strategies	Efficiency, Productivity, and Effectiveness
Business Understanding	Efficiency	All five strategies	Efficiency, Productivity, and Effectiveness
Workforce Acumen	Efficiency, Productivity, and Effectiveness	Efficiency, Productivity, and Effectiveness	Efficiency
Company Culture	Efficiency	All five strategies	Efficiency
Technology	Efficiency and Productivity	Efficiency, Productivity, and Effectiveness	Efficiency, Productivity, Effectiveness, and Growth
Data	Efficiency and Productivity	Efficiency and Productivity	All five strategies

For Company #1, the Efficiency-based AI strategy seems to be the dominant play. If they wanted, they could explore a "Productivity-based" strategy as a close second, but growth and expert-based strategies are out of the question; its too big of a stretch for their current maturity and team.

Company #2 can explore all the strategies; however, Efficiency and Productivity-based strategies seem to be their dominant plays. I would advise them to start here before getting into effectiveness, growth, or expert-based strategies.

For Company #3, the Efficiency-based AI strategy seems to be the dominant play. However, they've got both Effectiveness and Productivity as close seconds with growth as third. I would advise this company to have more discussions and explore their options, but I would advise them to lean into Efficiency as their first deployment if they can.

Knowing your dominant AI strategy is the first step to a successful AI deployment. It takes into account the reality of where you are as a leader, as a team, and as a company, and it will help you focus your ideation of use cases to things that you can feasibly deploy.

Phase 3: Creating and Selecting Use Cases

This is where the fun begins! In this chapter, we'll go through ways to ideate use cases that align with your AI strategy and discuss the criteria used to help you select your use case.

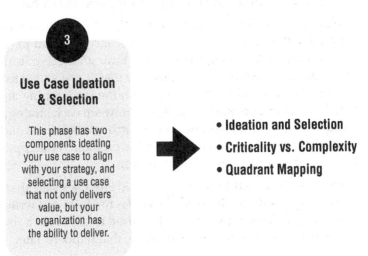

There are two parts to Phase 3: use case ideation and selection.

Ideation   This is where you and your team generate ideas and start capturing all the use cases that come to mind. No lengthy discussions are needed (at first). The primary goal is to think of use cases that you think align with your strategy, say them out loud, and write them down. The debate as to whether your use cases align with your dominant AI strategy doesn't happen just yet. Just ideate and capture!

Selection   Once all the ideas are written down and it's time to filter and select your use case, we'll go through a five-step exercise.

Use-Case Ideation

In Chapter 5 we will get into the details of your AI team and who should be in what meetings. For now, just know, in the ideation phase, you want to select your strategic thinkers, discerners, galvanizers, innovators, business partners, cofounders, or anyone else in your organization who has a growth-based mindset and can help ideate. You *don't* want to bring in the curmudgeons, or anyone who has a tendency of resisting change. You want a team that's generally excited about the possibilities new things bring and who can help you ideate, not those who are focused on job preservation or who fear change.

With this new group, you'll go through the following steps, either during a series of meetings or by knocking it out in a one-day workshop:

1. Explain your "why." Build the baseline knowledge for everyone, and clearly communicate the opportunity and the threat.

2. Explain the questionnaire and the realities of your current organizational maturity across the six sections and how that plays into your dominant AI strategy. Walk them through the five strategies, but spend the most time on the strategy that is best suited for your organization and why. Share with them the landscaping analogy to help them understand the nuances between each strategy. This will give everyone a direction, and a north star to follow, and help connect the dots between your business problems and opportunities with the strategy that's right for you.

3. Explain to them that they are here to ideate use cases that align with the dominant AI strategy. The goal is to ideate and write them all on a whiteboard. Do *not* use this time to debate if a use case aligns with your dominant AI strategy; that happens later.

4. Once you've explained everything, designate one person in the group who has the "veto" right to decide if a use case aligns with your AI strategy. Their job kicks in when we get into filtering the use cases in step 6.

5. Begin ideating! Let the ideas flow and write them all down. Remember, you're not filtering or discerning yet; just have an open dialogue of everything you want to fix or want to have in place that you *think* aligns with your dominant AI strategy.

6. Now that you've got everything written down, you will begin filtering the list.

   ▪ Go through the obvious use cases that don't align with your dominant AI strategy and cross them out. Notice how I said "obvious." These are the use cases where most of the folks in the room agree it's not fitting the definition of efficiency, productivity, effectiveness, expert, or growth. Minimal debate is usually had here because you're going for a majority vote. For example, if your dominant AI strategy is efficiency, you're not going to pick an SEO use case that's external facing and focused on growth, so cross that out.

- Then go through the use cases where there are questions on whether it aligns with your dominant AI strategy. There's usually a lot of debate here; expect it! Once a use case has been discussed *ad nauseum*, this is where your "veto" person kicks in. Have them make a judgment call for the sake of progress. Cross it out if it doesn't make the vetoer's list.

- Once you've crossed the use cases that don't align with your dominant AI strategy, create a new and clean list of the use cases that made it. This will be your running list to use in the selection process.

Use-Case Selection

I'm not a big believer in selecting use cases based on business value. I truly believe every use case or project has business value; it just depends on the lens, objective, and KPIs you're using to define business value.

What I like to do is take a quantitative approach that's rooted in practicality. I follow the process I invented when I was at IBM, that I've used at E&Y, and that I've used in all of my C-suite positions that's worked flawlessly once people understand the process and methodology. It's called the *Criticality vs. Complexity Quadrant.*

- **Criticality**   You're going to rate each use case (on a scale of 1 through 5) on how critical it is to the longevity, perseverance, and growth of your company.

- **Complexity**   You're going to rate each use case (on a scale of 1 through 5) on how difficult it will be to deploy the selected use case compared to other use cases.

In earlier chapters, I mentioned how AI deployments come in a variety of forms and with varying degrees of difficulty from really complex to straightforward. As such, when deciphering "complexity," we're assuming we're not doing any of the super-difficult, custom build stuff. We are going to leverage off-the-shelf AI tools built for consumer and/or enterprise use. Buying accelerates our time to market and makes the deployment a lot easier. I highly recommend this approach when you're first starting. I've created an image to help demonstrate what I mean:

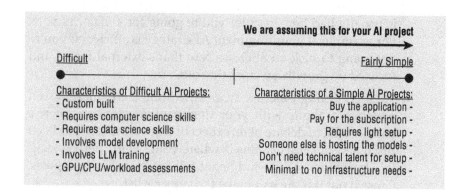

We are assuming this for your AI project

Difficult   Fairly Simple

Characteristics of Difficult AI Projects: Characteristics of a Simple AI Projects:
- Custom built   Buy the application -
- Requires computer science skills   Pay for the subscription -
- Requires data science skills   Requires light setup -
- Involves model development   Someone else is hosting the models -
- Involves LLM training   Don't need technical talent for setup -
- GPU/CPU/workload assessments   Minimal to no infrastructure needs -

How to Score Criticality and Complexity

For each of your use cases, you're going to answer six questions—three for criticality and three for complexity. Each answer will be rated on a scale of 1 through 5. When you're done, add up your scores. Your totals will range from 3 (minimum) through 15 (maximum). You'll then plot your use cases and their scores in a quadrant, as I have done here:

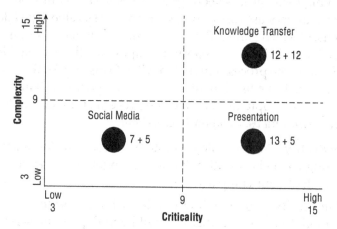

I'll give you step-by-step instructions on how to do this, but for now, the following are the 3 questions you'll be answering for Criticality and how you're going to rate them. For demonstration purposes, I provided example use cases that may have been generated during your ideation session. There are 3 distinct use cases (Social Media, Presentation, and Knowledge Transfer), and you're going to answer all 3 criticality questions for each use case.

Criticality

1. Does it, or can it, impact *sales and growth*?
   Example Use Case: Creating Decks
   "Creating a presentation for every new scope of work is really time-consuming and draining on the sales team. It's slowing us and our ability to respond quickly to requests. We lose momentum with prospects and existing clients, and we're not providing the service we promised."
   If this is your use case, you will go through and rate it (1 through 5) based on how you would answer the question. Write your score down.
   Rating of 1 = This has zero impact on us.

   Rating of 2 = This can have an impact but hasn't yet.

   Rating of 3 = This has had impacts on us, but not too frequent.

   Rating of 4 = We're starting to see the impacts because the occurrence is increasing, and issues are starting to arise.

   Rating of 5 = It's a critical problem for our organization.

2. Does it, or can it, impact *operations*?
   Example Use Case: Knowledge Transfer
   "We rely a lot on institutional knowledge. As a result, we have minimal documentation, and we are not very disciplined with our businesses process between our teams: sales, account management, and delivery. A lot of information is slipping through the cracks, and we're also not capturing the requirements well across all teams involved, wasting a ton of time in meetings and on email trying to figure things out."
   If this is your use case, go through and rate it (1 through 5) based on how you would answer the question. Write your score down.

   Rating of 1 = This has zero impact on us.

   Rating of 2 = This can have an impact but hasn't yet.

   Rating of 3 = This has had impacts on us, but not too frequent.

   Rating of 4 = We're starting to see the impacts because the occurrence is increasing, and issues are starting to arise.

   Rating of 5 = It's a critical problem for our organization.

3. Does it, or can it, impact *company culture* and *public perception*.
   Example Use Case: Social Media Content

"We're not the best at writing content, socializing our work, and coming across as thought leadership in our space. This has impacted our ability to hire and attract talent and make ourselves known in the marketplace. Most of our business comes from referrals, but it's not a sustainable model for the growth objectives we have this year and next."

If this is your use case, go through and rate it (1 through 5) based on how you would answer the question. Write your score down.

- Rating of 1 = This has zero impact on us.

- Rating of 2 = This can have an impact but hasn't yet.

- Rating of 3 = This has had impacts on us, but not too frequent.

- Rating of 4 = We're starting to see the impacts because the occurrence is increasing, and issues are starting to arise.

- Rating of 5 = It's a critical problem for our organization.

Now sum up the scores for each use case. At the end, you should have a Criticality score ranging from 3 (not critical at all) to 15 (very critical) for each use case.

Complexity

1. Does it impact *bandwidth* for other projects?
   Example Use Case: Creating Decks
   "Creating a presentation for every new scope of work is really time-consuming and draining on the sales team. It's slowing us and our ability to respond quickly to requests. We lose momentum with prospects and existing clients, and we're not providing the service we promised."
   If this is your use case, go through and rate it (1 through 5) based on how you would answer the question. Write your score down.

- Rating of 1 = We can take this on, no problem.

- Rating of 2 = We'll have to rearrange some things, but it's totally doable.

- Rating of 3 = This is going to impact us, so we'll need to coordinate with other teams to measure the degree of impact.

- Rating of 4 = We're stretched; something will have to give before we take on another strategic priority.

- Rating of 5 = This will break the team.

2. What is the degree of *change management* is needed?

    Example Use Case: Knowledge Transfer

    "We rely a lot on institutional knowledge. As a result, we have minimal documentation, and we are not very disciplined with our businesses process between our teams: sales, account management, and delivery. A lot of information is slipping through the cracks, and we're also not capturing the requirements well across all teams involved, wasting a ton of time in meetings and on email trying to figure things out."

    If this is your use case, go through and rate it (1 through 5) based on how you would answer the question. Write your score down.

    ▪ Rating of 1 = The team is clear on the value, and we're all ready to move forward.

    ▪ Rating of 2 = For the most part we're all aligned, but we'll need to spend some time up front to align folks.

    ▪ Rating of 3 = This is a mixed bag; we'll need to spend some time prepping and planning the teams.

    ▪ Rating of 4 = We have a lot of folks resisting change; they like the way things are.

    ▪ Rating of 5 = This will be an uphill battle, and it's a major change management effort.

3. Do we have clear *ownership* of this use case?

    Example Use Case: Social Media Content

    "We're not the best at writing content, socializing our work, and coming across as thought leadership in our space. This has impacted our ability to hire and attract talent and make ourselves known in the marketplace. Most of our business comes from referrals, but it's not a sustainable model for the growth objectives we have this year and next."

    If this is your use case, go through and rate it (1 through 5) based on how you would answer the question. Write your score down.

    ▪ Rating of 1 = We know which department or person should manage this.

    ▪ Rating of 2 = We have a few options; we can land on an owner fairly quickly, though.

    ▪ Rating of 3 = We can go a few routes; we'll need to discuss more with the team to assign an owner.

- Rating of 4 = This will be a lengthy discussion and may require leadership to make the final call.

- Rating of 5 = We have no idea which team or person can own this.

Now sum up the scores for each use case. At the end, you should have a Complexity score ranging from 3 (not critical at all) to 15 (very critical) for each use case.

	CRITICALITY			SUM	COMPLEXITY			SUM
	SCORE	SCORE	SCORE		SCORE	SCORE	SCORE	
1. Presentation for Clients	5	3	5	13	2	1	2	5
2. Knowledge Transfer	4	4	4	12	5	3	4	12
3. Social Media Outreach	2	1	4	7	2	2	1	5

As a basic illustration, I've created the following grid on the three sample use cases I provided earlier. I scored each question for each use case 1 through 5 and added the sum for Criticality and Complexity.

Now you plot the sums in a quadrant. The x-axis is Criticality (with the low scores to the left and the high scores to the right), and on the y-axis is Complexity (with the low scores on the bottom and the high scores on the top).

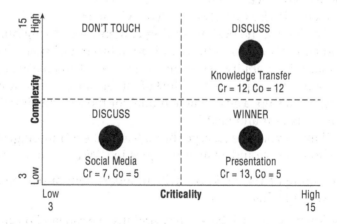

The use cases to the right will show your most critical use cases and where you feel your company will get the most value. In the previous illustration, "Knowledge Transfer" and "Presentations" clearly stand out.

Like with complexity, the use cases on the bottom half of the quadrant are simpler to deploy for you. In this case, "Social Media" and "Presentations" are the easiest for you to deploy.

Since "Presentations" is the only use case that's both critical and easiest to deploy (based on your maturity), you now have a use case that aligns with your dominant AI strategy. The use case is critical to your business, and is the least complex to deploy. *Voilà!*

NOTE This process of elimination will be your best friend on any project. It will avoid any lengthy discussions around the method used to calculate business value, personal feelings, and individual agendas. It's a clear and simple way to get alignment.

With the exercise now complete, there is a clear winner, and you have your use case!

Real-World and Practical Walk-Through

As you know already, I pride myself and have built my reputation, on being practical. So, the goal of this section is to walk you through a real-world simulation of how phases 1, 2, and 3 connect so you can see the flow and sequence of how things work. While I've provided the steps and framework for the "how to," I won't leave you high and dry with theory. Let's get on the bike and start riding so you can see how this plays out in real life. Let's role-play!

SUZANNE'S SCENARIO

My name is Suzanne, and I'm the CEO of a 200-person manufacturing firm, located in Kansas City, Missouri. We sell custom stainless-steel equipment to research labs, consumer product companies, and hospitals. Business is good, and demand is high, so I must invest in the company to expand its capacity to meet the incoming demand. I need to invest in steel-cutting and fabrication equipment so we can increase our output; however, I need a larger sales team to handle all the incoming leads. I can't turn away any business because I need to offset my investments in equipment with additional sales. Can AI help me with my sales team dilemma so I can focus my funds and investments on equipment?

Here's how the flow works (from Suzanne's viewpoint):

1. I've read Sol's book and I know my "why."

2. I've gone through Sol's questionnaire, it looks like our dominant AI strategy should be an Efficiency-based strategy. Why? Because:

- While I know our market, the company as a whole is mostly full of good-hearted operators. They are not thinking about the broader market shifts and threats.

- We are well intentioned, we look out for each other, but we're not disciplined with processes; we rely mostly on institutional knowledge and relationships to get the work done.

- I'm lucky to have my team since nearly everyone has a "can do" attitude. However, outside of our equipment operators, we don't really have specialists; most are generalists who figure things out on their own.

- We're definitely not shy with innovation; we're always up for figuring new things out.

- While tech does play a role within our company, it's specific to a few teams.

- I honestly have no idea about our data situation; we continue to grow, so I'm assuming everything is accessible and reliable.

3. I'm planning to have an ideation session, and I've decided to pull in my chief of staff, one of my investors, the head of sales, the head of product development, and a friend who runs a tech company as the ideation team. I sent them emails on what I want to do and that I was going to schedule a one-day off-site in two weeks to discuss our AI project and a few other things.

4. I had my chief of staff prepare a two-page document as a pre-read to our off-site meeting, and in it, we articulated the following:

- The state-of-the-union for our business and the promising fiscal year ahead of us, including the investments we need to make and the struggles we may run into if we don't plan and prepare now

- The purpose of the off-site and my "why"

- The exercises we're going to go through on ideation and selection and the methodology we're going to use so there's some sense of the plan before we all connect

- Clear outcomes for the off-site meeting

5. The off-site is scheduled, and everyone accepts.

6. On the day of the off-site, we get settled in and start immediately.

- I level set by explaining why I chose this team to lead this session and why I need their help.

- I explain my "why."

- I explain what I want to get out of this session.

- I cover the questionnaire, the five AI strategies, and why we're best suited for the efficiency-based strategy.

- Folks asked a bunch of clarifying questions; I answered them to the best of my knowledge, but I remind them that we're here to figure things out together. I'm just as new as they are to this.

- We go through and ideate a bunch of use cases and put them all on a whiteboard. It's messy at first, but we eventually get the hang of it. My chief of staff was great at keeping up with the ideas and writing them all down. This took us about 2.5 hours.

- We took a 20-minute break, and I heard a lot of buzz in the hallways.

- We all came back with a cup of coffee and started going through each use case, crossing off any use cases that weren't efficiency based. We had two use cases that we felt could be either efficiency-based or productivity-based, so we kept both; we didn't feel the need to over-debate anything.

7. After one hour of discernment, we crossed off what didn't fit, we finished the exercise, and landed on two use cases that were focused on creating efficiency for our sales team.

    Post-Meeting Notes: Find a way to reduce the time that sales reps spend on meeting notes, recaps, follow-ups, and action items after a client or prospect call. We've estimated the sales team spends on average 8–12 hours a week doing this work. This is time we can give back to help with lead generation and/or answering questions from new prospects.

    Presentation Creation: Find a way to reduce the time that sales reps spend on creating presentations for every client or prospect that wants new information, while also increasing the quality of the presentations. We feel we should be able to templatize things in a beautiful way without having to hire a graphic design team. We've estimated this will give the sales reps 10–13 hours back per week to help with lead generation and/or answering questions of new prospects.

8. We took a break for lunch and came back to run each of the two use cases through the criticality and complexity questions and scored each of them.

    Post-Meeting Notes: Had a 9 in criticality and a 6 in complexity.

    Presentations: Had a 9 in criticality and an 8 in complexity.

9. While both were fairly close with the scores, the team chose to move forward with Post-Meeting Notes because we felt many teams could benefit from this AI capability. It saves the sales team time, but it can also save time across many teams since we rely heavily on notes and emails (we're not very disciplined with our processes), and the complexity scores were fairly close, so we didn't think it would be an issue.

10. We ended our off-site meeting, and the next day my chief of staff sent out a post-meeting recap to all the attendees. We outlined our process, selection, and outcome. I've now asked my chief of staff to schedule a few follow-up meetings with the sales team to walk them through the off-site meeting outcomes and where we landed so we can properly prep for the design phase.

I hope this helped! It sure helped Suzanne.

Phase 4: Preparing and Designing

Now that you have a firm grasp of your use case, the next phase is the design phase. In this phase, the goal is to create a blueprint that will guide your teams in the direction you're headed by outlining and deciding on a bunch of things that go into AI project deployments.

Preparation & Designing

This step will help you create a blueprint that will outline your budget, resources, activities, tasks, and workflows. You choose the partnerships and technical expertise you need.

- 5 Categories
- **Vision, Impact, Process, Approach, and Support**
- **AI Pyramid of Scope**

Before we start, I want to provide some context into this chapter and the "AI Essentials Checklist" you will get in this chapter. Sorry to brag, but you won't find a more condensed and comprehensive list of practical to-dos anywhere. This is where my scraped knees, bruised elbows, wounded pride, and real-life deployment experience comes into play. Though it may feel lengthy, stick with it. The time you put into this up front will save you 20 times over later. It's a consolidated list of the most critical considerations and essentials for you and your team when planning your AI project specific to your use case, company, or industry.

For perspective, if I had to sum up the common mistakes I've witnessed in failed AI projects, they are the following:

- The first blunder is selecting the wrong use case, which we mitigated in phases 2 and 3.

- The second mistake is not knowing what to prepare for in advance, and it's why companies spend hundreds of thousands of dollars bringing in consultants who also don't have all the answers.

- The third mistake is not giving the preparation and design phase ample time. All of this fails to address crucial questions beforehand, leading to hasty problem-solving tactics during deployment, resulting in time-consuming, costly, and/or poor decisions.

We're going to mitigate the second and third reasons in phase 4 by giving you your very own "AI Essentials Checklist", which has five main categories as depicted here:

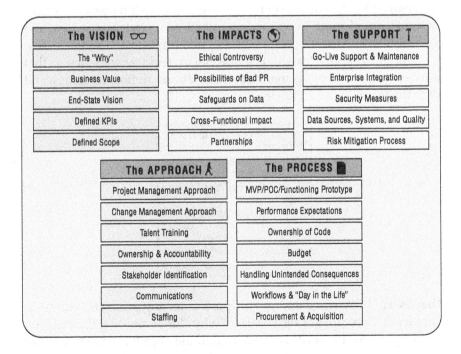

The VISION 👓	The IMPACTS 🕐	The SUPPORT ↑
The "Why"	Ethical Controversy	Go-Live Support & Maintenance
Business Value	Possibilities of Bad PR	Enterprise Integration
End-State Vision	Safeguards on Data	Security Measures
Defined KPIs	Cross-Functional Impact	Data Sources, Systems, and Quality
Defined Scope	Partnerships	Risk Mitigation Process

The APPROACH 𝗄	The PROCESS ■
Project Management Approach	MVP/POC/Functioning Prototype
Change Management Approach	Performance Expectations
Talent Training	Ownership of Code
Ownership & Accountability	Budget
Stakeholder Identification	Handling Unintended Consequences
Communications	Workflows & "Day in the Life"
Staffing	Procurement & Acquisition

The **vision** gives you direction and purpose so you can maximize engagement, set expectations, define outcomes, and align the team on the common goal.

The **impacts** help you understand and outline risks and impacts so that you can properly put in place decision rights, mitigation plans, and controls to reduce if not remove negative implications.

The **support** helps you define and decide the protocols for resolution that will help minimize downtime, resolve issues, safeguard your investments, and maintain the project's value over time.

The **approach** establishes a structured framework for overseeing your project execution and managing the transition as effectively as possible, while minimizing disruption to the business.

The **process** gives you a clear roadmap for resource allocation and needs, workforce responsibilities, and transparency into business processes. This will help bring clarity to the entire team, help avoid cost overruns, and foster team accountability.

Let's get into the details!

The Vision

The vision is the first and most crucial step in the design phase. You have thought through your "why" and identified your strategy, use case, and business value. Now it's time to validate and broadcast this information to the organization. This will provide clarity and transparency so that you can maximize engagement, set expectations, define outcomes, and align the team on the common goal.

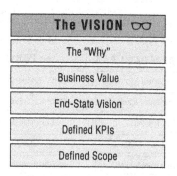

The "Why"   We discussed the purpose of asking yourself "why?" in Chapter 3. To recap, asking yourself "why?" is cementing the purpose of taking on AI. Regardless of your goal, the objective is to maximize business value, with minimal friction, and know why you're doing it. This may sound obvious, but as I mentioned, in my 20+ years of deployment experience, I have witnessed numerous instances where leaders and project teams have overlooked this step and gone straight into solutioning. Make sure you avoid this mistake and start with the "why" and share it with everyone. Be passionate about it. Be secure with it. Be confident with it (even if you're not at times).

Business Value   I won't teach you how to calculate business value. Many companies and organizations have their own methodology. Regardless of your techniques and method, do the work, make it available for everyone to see, and put it next to your "why." This is the second best way of evangelizing critical mass.

End-State Vision   This step may sound obvious too, but it's been interesting to witness how bad people are at describing their end-state vision. What does great look like? How would your day or life change if this were deployed successfully? What can or will it do for the company? Be detailed. Be descriptive. Don't be shy about what you envision. Think of Martin Luther King's "I Have a Dream" speech; no one captured end-state vision better than his speech. Don't be shy, and be just as colorful to get the team and organization mobilized and excited about your drive and vision as a leader.

Defined KPIs   Key performance indicators are a way for you to measure and manage the performance of an AI capability. It measures the outcome that matters to you and becomes a benchmark for tracking past, current, and future progress. In the case of Suzanne's use case, maybe some of her KPIs are: 1) "reduced time" in presentation creation, combined with 2) "average response time" for new scope of work requests, in addition to "increase in email replies" post-presentation. This way, you're measuring time spent, quality of the decks, and effectiveness via customer responses back to your presentation. The trick with KPIs, however, is that you *must* measure the current state, pre-AI, to have a benchmark of the business value your AI is creating. Do both a pre-measurement and a post-measurement. Without it, you have nothing to compare it to, and your argument for the benefits of AI fall apart.

Defined Scope   This too is obvious, but the biggest mistake made here with AI projects is the scope is either over-generalized and doesn't get into essential details or the scope focuses on the solution and not the other essential areas. Whereas when you're preparing a scope document that serves as a blueprint for solutioning and gaining critical mass, it should include what I've outlined for you in my "The AI Pyramid of Scope." The scope document should always include the following:

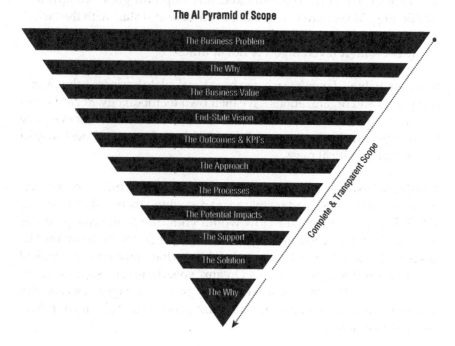

The AI Pyramid of Scope

- The Business Problem
- The Why
- The Business Value
- End-State Vision
- The Outcomes & KPI's
- The Approach
- The Processes
- The Potential Impacts
- The Support
- The Solution
- The Why

Complete & Transparent Scope

This becomes your manifesto for every team, teammate, vendor, partner, or investor you're onboarding.

The Impacts

This section is about proactively discussing and identifying any negative impact on your customers, teammates, or public perception of what you're doing. This is unique to AI for sure. After all, who starts a project discussing negative impacts? No one. However, with AI projects, it's a critical step in preparation.

As we know, AI is not perfect. Humans are not perfect. Everyone and everything has the potential to make mistakes, and we need to be aware of the mishaps and unintentional consequences early on. Outline what we think could be impacts, and outline how to prepare for it.

As it stands today, AI can hallucinate, AI can concatenate real facts to create unrelated facts, it's disrupting industries and functions, and it's creating a crop of new AI-based companies that's gobbling up market share. As a result, AI is creating a visceral reaction in people and companies because of its power and imperfections. As such, it's important we think through all the negative implications so that we can get ahead of any bad press or PR, both within your company and externally.

Therefore, discuss the following with your team:

Ethical Controversy   Could there be any risks associated with cultural, cognitive, or computational bias with your solution? Technically, if you're buying something off-the-shelf, they should have worked through most of that, but it's never perfect. That's why it's important for you to think through and test for biases before releasing anything. Always have a "human in the loop," We'll discuss more of this in Chapter 6.

Bad PR   Does your use case imply bad practices that could attract negative attention? Examples include discriminating in your talent recruitment, reselling data, using AI in judicial systems or for credit scoring, diagnosing health, or conducting invasive surveillance. While I'm sure the intent is never to cause harm, the goal here is really to think through what could or may happen.

Safeguards on Data   Identify any risks associated with data. For example, are you inadvertently touching personal or sensitive data, like PII classified data? Could you be collecting it? Could you be storing it? If so, what safeguards need to be put in place to abide by any regulations?

Cross-Functional Impacts   Think through what teams, what functions, and which individuals will be impacted with the introduction of this new capability. How do their jobs change? Will they be re-allocated to other teams; if so, when do you communicate, and when do you prepare them? You'll need to think through who's more sensitive to change and how to best incorporate a plan for them within your change management approach.

Partnerships   As we all know, bad partnerships of any kind (relationships, friendships, and marriages) can have negative impacts on us. As such, its important you outline what you want in a partner if you choose to get outside help. Choosing the wrong partner can delay deployment, increase costs, delay benefits, create suboptimal performance, and, worse, lower morale. Always get references.

The Approach

This section is all about ensuring you've thought through and have well-defined approaches that provide a structured framework for planning, executing, and monitoring your AI project so that you deploy on time and on budget, keep morale and team engagement high, and get the value and outcomes you originally sought. That's easier said than done, right?

> **NOTE**   The good news is that most projects don't fail because of bad intentions; most projects fail because of bad planning. That's why I encourage you to think slow in order to act fast.

As mentioned earlier, the length and degree to which you plan are very dependent on your personal style and company culture. If you're simply buying a monthly subscription to a tool called SuperOtter.AI for you and three teammates to capture meeting notes during Zoom conference calls, you don't need to go through all of this in great detail. However, if you are a company of 100 and you're automating the tasks of a team of 23, you'll need to go through most of this, but maybe not in excruciating detail. If, however, you work in an enterprise or private company that generates a few billion in annual revenue and you're in a conservative industry such as insurance, manufacturing, legal, or healthcare, you're going to want to go through *all* of this, and in detail, to make sure you've thought through everything.

So, use your own discretion for the level of detail that needs to be discussed, planned, and documented for each of these seven areas covered under the approach. Whatever you do, though, don't skip any of them. Even if the answer is "Nothing," "N/A," or Not Applicable," discuss it and write your response down with the team you've assembled.

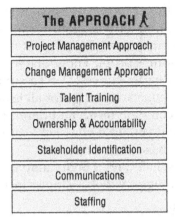

Project Management Approach   Whether you follow waterfall, agile, hybrid, or ad hoc, outline how you're going to do things. A list of project management tasks and activities that are essential for AI projects are included here. Feel free to add more, but don't skip any of these, please:

- Project charter (include everything we discussed under the vision)
- Milestones and deliverables
- Schedule and timing
- Resource needs, roles, and responsibilities
- Budget tracking
- Work breakdown of tasks and subtasks
- Risk and issue tracking, logging, and resolutions
- Status reports to stakeholders, teams, and cross-functional teams
- Conflict resolution and triaging
- Project documentation and storage (Notion, Confluence, Microsoft Teams, Google Docs)

Change Management Approach   Change management is tricky, especially if you've never formally done it before or if you have a company that has a habit of talking about its importance yet always short-changes its investments on projects. Since change management has a lot to do with the "people" side of things, I provide another essential checklist in Chapter 5, where we focus on people.

Talent Training   For this approach, the goal is to ensure anyone who needs training, upskilling, or basic knowledge gets the education, exposure, and support they need. The biggest mistake you can make on an AI project is to assume people know, understand, or have studied the subject area—including executives. Don't assume that! Take the time to level-set, build a baseline knowledge for all teams and stakeholders involved, and create common terms and definitions. Talent training and workshops will trip you up if you skip over this step. I've seen it happen far too many times.

As an example, I host half-day AI Boot Camp workshops for all executives. I walk them through a variety of topics including the following:

- What AI is and is not
- Terms and definitions
- Opportunities and threats
- Facts versus fiction
- Value generation versus deterioration
- Roles and responsibilities
- Why AI projects fail
- What to expect
- What we need from you

This brings everyone together and level-sets knowledge and expectations. I've provided a training list here. You may not need all of it, but work with your team and decide what is needed and to what extent.

- Needs assessment (who needs training)
- Audience (create your target audience and what they need to learn or know)
- Curriculum development
- Knowledge store and materials (videos, documents, manuals)
- Training method (in-person, virtual, web)
- Scheduling and logistics (block calendars as early as you can)
- Participation registration and tracking (track who's attended, finished, or absent)
- Feedback loop and assessment (gather feedback; this is a good indication of where people's concerns might be)

Ownership and Accountability   This sounds simple, but depending on the size of your organization, organizational model, culture, and cross-functional dependencies, this can get really complicated, really quickly. Here's a simple diagram to illustrate the degrees of difficulty in deciding ownership and accountability for your AI project:

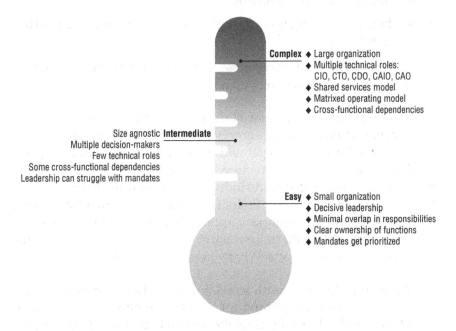

Complex ◆ Large organization
◆ Multiple technical roles:
  CIO, CTO, CDO, CAIO, CAO
◆ Shared services model
◆ Matrixed operating model
◆ Cross-functional dependencies

Size agnostic **Intermediate**
Multiple decision-makers
Few technical roles
Some cross-functional dependencies
Leadership can struggle with mandates

Easy ◆ Small organization
◆ Decisive leadership
◆ Minimal overlap in responsibilities
◆ Clear ownership of functions
◆ Mandates get prioritized

Even if you have stakeholders, executive sponsors, peer groups, and/or multiple teams connecting on AI, groupthink does not cancel out single tracked ownership. Just like you need a captain and a crew to sail a ship, a driver and passengers for every road trip, and a quarterback to make calls for a team that relies on both offensive and defensive teams, you need an assigned leader who will have ownership and accountability for your AI project. This is a common mistake companies make; they think sharing responsibility works for AI projects.

Stakeholder Identification   For an AI project to be successful, the composition and quality of a stakeholder will really make a difference for you if you're in a highly political or sensitive culture. A well-chosen stakeholder group provides support, resources, and guidance, and most of all, it clears the runway for you. This last point has always been the most valuable for me. It truly does make your life easier when you have someone who believes in you and what you're doing. This is why, when selecting stakeholders, don't just accept any executive. Spend time and look for the right one. Invest time in convincing them to take this on and look for the following attributes:

- They have decision-making authority.
- They are change champions.
- They will be engaged in both decision-making and conflict resolutions.

It's that simple. If you have those three qualities among your stakeholders, you have everything you need.

Communications   Having a well-documented and executive communication plan sounds obvious; however, you'd be amazed at how loose, lazy, or lackadaisical teams get with following through on their plan. While the goal is to have a structured approach to ensure stakeholders, project teams, the company, and individuals are informed, where things fall apart on AI projects is the discipline in recommunicating the "vision" expected outcomes with impact, approach, process, and the solution. We tend to just stick with status reports, and that's not a great communication plan for AI projects. What you need is the following:

Vision and Objective Setting   Malcolm Gladwell once said it takes 6 times to repeat something for it to be remembered and nearly 23 times to repeat something for the content to be heard. Don't assume everyone understood the vision the first time you communicated it. Restate it. When you think you're done, repeat it all over again.

Key Messages   Communicate progress, outcomes, risks, impacts, milestones, and more.

Select Your Communications Channels and Formats   Decide if you're doing email, videos, in-person, virtual, etc. The answer will likely be all depending on the group you're communicating too.

Audience of Communication   Who do you need to communicate with? What do they want to know? How often should you communicate?

Feedback and Solicitation   Plan for what stage in the project you intend to get feedback and solicitation and what you're going to do with it.

Training and Support   Decide if you're going to host training sessions, write how-to guides, and establish a help desk. Who's going to be your point of contact? Do you need to set up an email address for inquiries?

KPIs and Metrics   While not all companies do this, you may choose to make your KPIs and metrics public so people aren't relying on heresy to form an impression of the business benefits; they can see them for themselves.

Staffing   This one is tricky! Your approach for how to staff your AI project will change slightly depending on whether you get to build your team or you must work with an existing team and taskforce. We discuss this more in Chapter 5, but without giving away too much, just know that your people can be your project killers or project makers. So, how you staff is critical. The team's eagerness, grit, ambition, and work ethic are the key attributes for deploying any small or large project with success. It's the attitude of the team and how the team gels that really brings it all together. Here's how to think about staffing in the two scenarios:

You get to build a team   This is the situation you want to be in if given the choice. Hand select individuals who have a track record for driving change, have a "can-do" attitude, and are gritty, ambitious, and resilient. Surround yourself with reliable and hungry people so that the weight and burden doesn't fall completely on your shoulders. You need other rogue leaders with you regardless of their level or role. Remember, going rogue is a mindset, not a title, and you need other like-minded individuals to make it a success. While most of you may be tempted to hire an outside person with expertise, I think there's great potential in finding someone internally who has the interest, aptitude, and work ethic to figure it out. Don't overlook finding people from within your team.

You inherit a team   This gets tricky as you may get a mixed bag of personalities. Some may be complacent, overly critical, or simply resistant. Others could be optimistic and excited to be at the forefront of something impacting society. In Chapter 5, I've outlined in detail the 10 AI archetypes and how to best deal with them so that you don't sabotage your project before you even start.

Skillset Alignment   Technical skills aside, make sure the folks you bring on board can drive the project forward either because of their subject matter expertise or because of their rogue mindset.

Specialization   Staff the team with a blend of experienced professionals who can help solve complexities and conflict.

Team Dynamics   Remove or reduce the possibility of having any cowboys or lone rangers on the team. This will be a team sport, so you have to avoid that personality type.

Your Staffing Model   You're going to have a core team helping you with solutioning and deployment. However, save approximately 30% of your budget to scale up, scale across, or scale down depending on unforeseen complexities or changing use cases. While this rarely happens because of the preparation involved in phases 1, 2, and 3, it can happen. Your team will also likely comprise full-time, part-time, and contracted employees and consultants, so you'll need to manage the opex and capex associated with building this asset.

Evaluations and Adjustments   This is the least favorite part of my job, but also necessary. If it's a small project and you're simply buying something off the shelf, you likely won't need to make staffing adjustments. Your project is straightforward, short in duration, and low risk. If, however, your use case is a bit more complicated, you'll need to put in place some guardrails around when and how you'll assess the team and progress. The best advice I can give you is, don't let a bad apple rotten the basket. You must be decisive and take action if you know someone is pulling the project down. Be deliberate in your thinking but swift in your decision, and act.

The Process

This section is all about ensuring you've outlined, documented, and reviewed the processes associated with a variety of areas such as current-state and to-be state workflows, ownership of activities, procurement protocol, and reviews. The goal is to ensure team members are aligned with project goals, methodologies, and expectations and to make sure there is consistent application of practices. This enables effective project management, onboarding of resources, and monitoring. Without processes in place, your project is susceptible to scope creep, confusion, miscommunication, and inconsistencies in how things should be executed, all resulting in delays and costs.

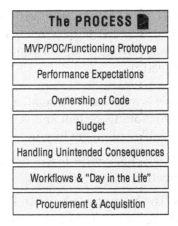

The PROCESS
MVP/POC/Functioning Prototype
Performance Expectations
Ownership of Code
Budget
Handling Unintended Consequences
Workflows & "Day in the Life"
Procurement & Acquisition

MVP/POC/Functioning Prototype

Deciding on your outcome and the form and function in which it takes is the most difficult step in designing (in my humble opinion). As a team you have to decide what you want your outcome to be and accept the advantages and disadvantages that come with each of the three option outlined here:

Minimum Viable Product (MVP)   This is the most pared-down version of a "live" product. It includes core features and services to provide immediate value to the business, knowing more iterations and advancements will be needed.

- ■ **Advantages:** Quick market entry, quick feedback loop, cost-effective
- ■ **Disadvantages:** Limited functionality (only the core), misunderstanding of scope by business users (they often think it's the full product and expect it to better), and brand risk (if it's too minimal in nature)

Functioning Prototype (FP)   A functioning prototype is a working model of the product that demonstrates how the capability would work under real-life conditions. It's more comprehensive than a POC, including both core and additional features, but it's not market-ready

- ■ **Advantages:** Good litmus test for evaluation, good way to get stakeholder engagement and company alignment, quickly identifies areas for improvement

- **Disadvantages:** Higher costs, takes more time, potential for wastage due to mismatched expectations (because business users think the product is ready and won't understand needing more time to make it market-ready)

Proof of Concept   This is meant to be a small exercise to test your use case. It is not a fully functioning system and is used mostly to demonstrate the art of the possible and to get buy-in.

- **Advantages:** Quick check with feasibility to deploy, and quick alignment in direction and expectations
- **Disadvantages:** The biggest gotcha with POCs is that they often take too long, losing the attention span and support of the powers that be. You also have to deal with not knowing how the "live" product will operate within your organization, it doesn't provide insight into user experience (since it's not a fully functioning product), and it might not account for real-world complexities

While all three options are available to you, as a general rule it's best to go down the MVP route with smaller projects that are focused on either an efficiency, productivity, or effectiveness strategy with your AI projects. However, as the project increases in complexity and your strategy is expert or growth based, creating FPs or POCs is a better route so you don't unnecessarily put something in production that you'll regret.

Performance Expectations   With AI projects, not every attempt leads to a product or process that goes live in production, so remove those expectations. Like humans, AI is not perfect. If what the AI produces doesn't meet your minimum requirements, as you have identified them, you can't go live with the solution. That's why it's important you outline your performance expectations up front and iterate until you get there. This may take several attempts.

As an example, when Watson was helping provide personalized treatment plans for patients who had cancer, we had this concept called *coefficient levels*, which essentially operated as our confidence level for suggested treatments. If Watson had a coefficient level of 70% or higher, it would provide the answer to the question. If, however, its coefficient level was less than 70%, it was programmed not to give an answer to avoid misinformation. You need to take a similar approach. Determine what is good enough and document it clearly. This way, when you begin testing, you know what your go/no-go threshold is for your project.

Another important aspect to performance is data. I can write an entire book on data; however, I'm going to spare you the details and make it relevant only to your AI project. It's well known that you need good data to produce quality and performant AI results. However, most companies aren't blessed with clean, accessible, or sizable data. That's why in phase 1, I asked you to answer two questions on your data situation. If you don't have quality, accessibility, or volume, your strategy for AI is limited to running with either an efficiency-based or productivity-based strategy. Both categories can run without massive data dependencies. Furthermore, we are going with off-the-shelf solutions and not custom-built models or LLMs as your first set of AI projects so you're clear of the data burden.

Ownership of Code   This is less relevant for you since I've suggested leveraging an off-the-shelf solution for your first project. I suggest you not build custom code of any type. However, there may be instances where you will need to integrate an API into the software or integrate your AI application with existing databases. In that case, make sure you identify among your team internally or externally who is going to write and maintain the code in production.

Budget   Outline the process of how you're going to track budget. If it's a simple project that involves purchasing a license and you are billed monthly, the process is easy. If, however, your AI project involves multiple teams, contractors, a variety of SaaS-based software solutions that need to be integrated, and cloud costs, you need to document all sources for cost. Make the decision on who has ownership rights over the numbers presented, and don't forget to bake in full-time employee costs (opex), and cloud costs. These are two areas often left out because the cost implications aren't so obvious.

Handling Unintended Consequences   Chapter 6 walks through in detail how to handle unintended consequences. In that chapter I share a not so funny, but funny, personal story of AI gone wrong and the unintended consequences that were experienced by the company and myself. While most situations are avoidable, some happen because a decision is made in haste or there wasn't a "human in the loop." Therefore, it is best that you discuss what the process would be in case there is an unintended consequence. How should the team be informed? Who gets pulled in? What's the timeline for deciding? Who has ownership of rectifying the situation, and what parties are involved? The goal is to be prepared, just in case!

Workflows and "Day in the Life"   Regardless of your AI strategy, you'll want to review, document, and outline your current business process that's under review so that when you evolve or adapt to a new process with your AI project, you have clarity in the following:

- Your existing processes and who owns what
- Team checkpoints and handoffs
- Roles and responsibilities with completing tasks and activities
- Source systems and destination systems in the mix
- Who has quality control rights

This helps bring transparency to how things are done today, which allows you to highlight the gaps and opportunities you'd like to address when solutioning your new AI project. This will help you establish new performance thresholds and KPIs, allowing you to measure business value.

Procurement and Acquisition   In reality, if you're a business leader or business owner running a small business, the process of purchasing the license or software of an AI application will be straightforward. You'll find your off-the-shelf solution, create an account, pay with a corporate card, activate the account, and off you go. But in two of my earlier deployments, I was caught off guard because I was unaware we had to pull in procurement, and it delayed both my projects by nearly three months. These are the common mistakes I see:

- You don't know the role procurement plays so you don't include them.
- You pull them too late into the process.
- The department has other competing priorities, and they don't have enough time to review everything in a timely manner.
- SOWs and MSAs become complex because "data" is involved so legal counsel needs to be pulled in, delaying things further.
- The department is small, so the workload of one or two individuals is too great to meet your project timelines.

The point I'm trying to make here is that it's important to get all your key stakeholders involved early in the process and to not overlook the procurement team. I've stepped into a lot of hot water by overlooking this team, accidentally of course.

The Support

Continuing the theme of making sure you're prepared and thinking through your AI project, you'll also have to discuss and decide on your support activities after you go live.

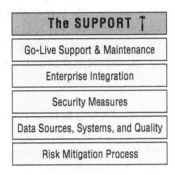

While a majority of these decisions will be made in phase 5 while you're solutioning, it's important you build a running list so you leave no stone unturned. Also, remember that the extent to which you discuss, decide, and document depends on your leadership style and company culture.

Go-Live Support and Maintenance   Once your AI application has gone live, you'll need to support and maintain the environment. This can be a simple process if you bought an off-the-shelf solution. You don't have to maintain any code or environments; all you are doing is logging into your account and checking the dashboard.

Enterprise Integration   If your use case requires you to pull in data from your customer relationship manager (CRM) system, cross-reference data with your financial system, manage user roles, or integrate with your media agencies software, you'll need to think through how to design your integration. Make sure you document the following:

- Integration overview, purpose, and outcome
- System landscape
- Integration requirements
- Data models and structures
- Security protocols
- API specifications
- Error handling and logging

- Testing strategy
- Monitoring and tooling
- Rollback and recovery

If what I just outlined here seems overly technical and you are not familiar with some of these terms, just know as a business leader that you're not expected to do the work yourself. However, make sure you know about the items on the previous list and hand it off to your "technical person," whether it be someone internal or external, to make sure they are thinking through it.

> **NOTE** Integrations can unintentionally become a big factor in your AI project. Why? If you purchase a pipeline tool to integrate your CRM data to your AI off-the-shelf solution and your CRM goes through an upgrade, you can break the integration between your CRM data and AI tool. Be aware of this in advance and plan for it.

Security Measures   The same applies with security. You're not expected to have all this in place if your use cases are simple. However, if your use case is a bit more complicated and it requires integrations with other systems or applications, make sure you hand this checklist to your "technical" person so they cover these essentials:

- Policy on how to handle PII or sensitive data
- Network security protocols
- Authentication and authorization process
- Encryption process
- API security
- Security tools and monitoring
- Disaster recovery
- Hardware or cloud surveillance

Data Sources, Systems, and Quality   For use cases that have data dependencies, you'll need to prepare for and design for the following areas:

- Data sources and inventory
- Data flow diagrams
- Mapping and transformation logic
- Data cleansing and validation procedures
- Data governance policies

- Data storage and retention policies
- Accessibility
- Quality thresholds

> **NOTE**   A word of caution: please don't be overwhelmed by the previous lists. I know it appears to be a lot, especially with everything outlined in phase 4 so far. Just remember, the goal is to make sure you're 100% prepared no matter how simple or complex your use case is through the lessons I've learned. You ultimately decide what's relevant and discuss it as a team if you don't know.

Risk Mitigation Process   In the prior sections, we discussed negative impacts, handling unintended consequences, security measures, and a go-live support checklist. All of this will culminate into a risk mitigation plan that needs to be followed when you go live. You'll need to outline roles and responsibilities, your communication plan, and how to evaluate situations.

That wraps up phase 4, the design phase. We discussed the five key areas that are essential for your success in your AI project, from defining a clear and compelling vision to understanding potential impacts, choosing approaches, implementing effective processes, and ensuring you have the right support system in place.

However, I'm sure by now you feel overwhelmed, remember, if you were learning to ride a bike, the instruction manual detailing every nuance of balance, pedaling, steering, and safety could also appear intense and overwhelming. Yet, much like riding a bike, navigating through an AI project often becomes more intuitive and natural than it seems on paper. You just have to do it to understand it!

As you move forward into phase 5, solutioning, keep in mind that the key to success with AI lies in open dialogue and preparedness. While manuals serve as a guide, the real learnings come from doing. So, take these essential checklists, guides, and toolkits as a roadmap rather than a hurdle, and you'll see how naturally things will align.

Phase 5: Selecting a Solution

Now that we've properly prepped and put together a design, the next phase is solutioning. This is where we align our designs with a tool of choice and begin deploying.

Solutioning

The solution phase is
about how you turn
your designs into reality.
This is where you
research your AI tools
and partner with
the technical expertise
you need.

- Tool Selection
- Off-the-Shelf, Off-the-Model, Off-the-LLM
- Interoperability with experts
- SOPs

There are two main aspects to phase 5: selecting a tool and making sure it is a good choice based on your experts.

Tool Selection   There are a few key decision points to be made when selecting a tool. The first decision is whether you should build a custom solution or buy an off-the-shelf solution. The second is researching your technical options. Third is assessing how the options align with the expected outcome of your vision.

Interoperability with Your Experts   Your solution must always involve the people you trust and those who understand the business problem and domain. Examples include your customer support specialists, sales reps, field technicians, and clinicians. No matter the use case, your employee experts and users best understand where the breakdowns, inefficiencies, product breakdowns, customer sensitivities, and ineffectiveness occur within the day to day, which gets captured in phase 4, under "Workflows and Day in the Life."

Tool Selection

AI technology has matured exponentially in recent years, and with the advent of cloud solutions, software-as-a-service (SaaS), and AI-ready consumer-facing products, finding solutions and adopting AI is easier than ever. Compared to what I had to go through back in 2011 and up until recently, the breakthroughs are astounding. The options are vast today, but I've summarized them into three categories:

The first decision we need to make is whether to custom build a solution or buy an off-the-shelf solution. As we've discussed in prior chapters, I highly recommend you stay away from custom building your own solution. Stay to the far left of this graph and go with off-the-shelf unless you're a Google, OpenAI, Anthropic, AWS, or a tech-based company with loads of cash and can attract highly sought after tech talent.

Why do I suggest this? To leverage the benefits of AI, there's no longer a need to invest in hiring data scientists, developers, or machine learning experts, and upping your infrastructure to support the workloads and models. We'll cover the topic of skillsets more later. For now, just know that much more qualified individuals have solved the problems for us in the off-the-shelf solutions and have created consumer-friendly products that are ready to use.

As such, I say be grounded in practicality and leverage the solutions that are off-the-shelf and utilize any number of solutions to:

- Analyzing large sets of data for insights
- Summarizing contracts and documents
- Recap online meetings and automate the process of sending follow-up notes and action items
- Translate your marketing campaigns from one language to another
- Templatize and automate the creation of decks for client presentations.
- Photo edit head shots, images, and content

Off-the-shelf solutions are available for nearly everything. It's just a matter of researching the options and seeing what best aligns with your needs. To give you more context and make you feel at ease, let's discuss what's available and why the market shifted in this direction.

AI Solutions and Tools

Nearly 10 to 15 years ago, AI technology was a resource exclusive to large-scale corporations; its capabilities were largely concentrated on serving the business-to-business (B2B) sector. The landscape has dramatically shifted, though, thanks to OpenAI. AI is now democratized, expanding its reach beyond the confines of B2B and directly catering to consumers (D2C). This transition has opened up a suite of tools that were previously inaccessible to us, the masses.

Now, at this very moment in time, we're hearing a lot about large language models (LLMs) and how everyone can train these models for personalized business use cases. However, training LLMs is time-consuming and expensive, requires technical talent, and requires an investment in infrastructure. This is unnecessary, in my opinion, especially with the way things are shaping up today. The AI landscape is evolving at breakneck speed, and within it is a vast array of prebuilt tools designed for immediate application and aimed at accelerating your AI initiatives.

My point of view is to leverage these tools. The tools are available and primed for immediate integration by you and your team. While the tools are easier to integrate, please don't expect a "plug-and-play" situation. Even with off-the-shelf solutions, they require brainstorming, critical thinking, the process of redesigning existing processes, governance, iterations, and quality control (QC). That's why it's important you go through all the phases I outlined in this chapter. Please don't skip anything.

Also, while everyone can leverage AI at a pace perhaps never seen before as a result of AI tools becoming available to the average person at a very low cost (I've seen costs as low as $9.99/user to $39.99/user and many have free trials for 14 days), there's something to keep in mind: the longevity of these companies.

Venture capital investments in AI-based companies have expanded sixfold, creating an influx of startups and scale-ups entering the market. This surge is great as it gives us options. However, it also introduces a degree of uncertainty with the longevity of these companies. While there's an AI solution for virtually every labor-intensive business task, the longevity of these AI-based companies is not certain. Many may not surpass the critical two-year start-up mark. So, while the potential for rapid advancement using AI tools is substantial, it's accompanied by the inherent risks associated with the longevity of these companies.

With that said, it's still a no-brainer: you should get started now and begin your AI journey leveraging the myriad of tools available in the marketplace. In the following sections, I'll list the tools I've used personally or are familiar with that can help you get started. Please be aware, though; in no way shape or form am I being paid or sponsored by these companies. I am 100% vendor agnostic. I'm only sharing the tools I've touched to help you get started. Regardless, the point is that the following chart will give you a head start in your research and let you know there are countless options out there.

I've categorized AI solutions into eight categories and highlighted a few companies within each.

SUMMARIZING CALLS, NOTES, AND ACTION ITEMS	CREATING DECKS AND PRESENTATIONS	CONTENT CREATION AND WRITING
Otter.AI	Tome.Ai	EliteAI Writer
SuperNormal.com	Gamm.app	Hyperwriteai.com
Semply.AI	Beautfiul.ai	Ryterme.ai
Leexi.AI	Decktopus.com	TextCortex.com
Spinach.Io	SlidesBean.ai	Quillbot.com
DOCUMENT REVIEWS, GUIDES, AND SOP CREATION	**IMAGE GENERATION FOR WEBSITES AND CONTENT**	**WEB TRAFFIC AND OPTIMIZATION**
Mintlify.com	Galileo.ai	Optimizely.com
Scribehow.com	Jasper.ai	Clearscope.Io
Bearly.ai	PepperType.ai	Semrush.com
Afforai.com	Stockimg.ai	MarketMuse.com
Super.ai	UiMagic.io	SurferSeo.com
UIPath.com	AdCreative.ai	CanIRank.com
CharterWorks.AI	Nightcafe Creator	GetPenny.com
CHATBOTS AND SALES AGENTS	**SALES CONVERSIONS AND MARKETING**	**CHATBOTS AND SALES AGENTS**
Forethought.ai	Opinly.ai	Dante-ai.com
Quickchat.ai	Frontnow.com	Chatbase.co
Typewise.app	Customers.AI	Sprinklr.co
Liveperson.com	Octaneai.com	Chatsimple.ai

As an example, I can't tell you how many hours I've spent in Corporate America building decks—decks that are visually appealing or decks that are elegant, simple, and with the right level of content that showcased my narrative. Sometimes for really important presentations like with the board or for a pitch to investors. On average I could easily spend 30–80 hours on a deck. But with software like Gamma App, I can create first-draft decks in less than 30 minutes that hit the mark. My effort then becomes focused on the narrative and not formatting and visuals (which can be very time-consuming).

Another time-consuming activity that I've personally automated is meeting minutes and follow-ups. During my formative years as a delivery lead, project manager, or partner, client meetings were very important. It's where we got feedback and tracked action items, risks, assumptions, and activities. But it was hard to listen and capture the feedback. Also, when the call ended, I would have to go through all my notes, organize them into an email, PowerPoint file, or Word document; proofread it; and send it out hoping I didn't leave anything out or make a mistake. That exercise alone would take me nearly 45–90 minutes. However, now I'm automating the whole process with the solutions I mentioned above so I can be more present during the calls, avoid multitasking, and send the notes out quickly. While I proofread everything, the summary and notes are nearly accurate, and I'm able to reduce my 45–90 minutes to 10–15 minutes.

In short, these off-the-shelf AI solutions will help your use case, but they can help you personally too by becoming more efficient, effective, and productive.

Steps for the Selection Process

To make things easier for you, I've outlined steps for you to follow so that you know the sequence of events that occurs when researching, selecting, and activating your off-the-shelf AI solution. They are as follows:

1. Research your off-the-shelf options. You can either do this internally with your existing team or hire a consultant or a firm to do it for you.

2. Assess your options against what you documented in phase 4. Take your current business process, business rules, and checkpoints and map them against the tool to assess opportunities, limitations, and constraints for each tool. Review the constraints in detail.

While there are tons of benefits, not all tools are built the same, so you're going to assess both the business benefits and the limitations and do a classic risk/reward analysis.

3. Review the pricing models of each option. If you were to scale it past individual licenses, how would it scale to multiple users and business processes across the organization?

4. Become familiar with their security protocols and data privacy protocols and assess the safety of their environment. Are they a startup with minimal safety measures, or are they a scale-up with enterprise-grade security protocols?

5. Review the user experience. Assess how easy it is to use, how easy would it be to adopt, and if it requires intense training or is it intuitive.

6. Does it solve for an individual task or can it scale to solve an entire business process from end to end? If it doesn't scale, review the product roadmap to see if there are valuable features and functionality that would be of benefit.

7. Assess how cumbersome the support needs are on your team post go-live. Is it self-service, or will you need a services team?

8. Ask these questions about the company:
   - How many years have you been in business?
   - How many clients are currently on your platform?
   - Do you have any enterprise logos?
   - Which VCs and investors are backing you?
   - Who do you have as advisors?

The goal is to assess their longevity so when you make the investment, you can feel good about their staying power.

Once you're done with all eight steps with your team, compile your assessments, review the results with your employees and experts, narrow down your results, and select your tool of choice.

Interoperability with Your Experts

After you've selected your tool, your subject-matter experts become critical in outlining the new standard operating procedure for your AI enablement. This entails creating step-by-step outlines and procedures for how your workers are to carry out a process leveraging your new AI tool. It entails documenting the procedure and creating a diagram of how the work is to be executed.

Here is an example of a SOP diagram:

PURPOSE

This SOP boosts Positive Charge's search engine rankings and visibility, thereby increasing the company's target audience.

KEYWORDS AND DEFINITIONS

KEYWORD	DEFINITION

SCOPE

This SOP applies to the digital marketing team members who are responsible for SEO.

PROCEDURE

Check the SEO rankings, traffic, and analytics.
Assess the on and off-page optimization.
Promote high-performing digital content.
Update the digital content for optimization.
Check and resolve 404 errors.
Review 301 redirects.
Schedule .txt file updates.
Schedule and run reports.
Update the schema markup.
Conduct search tests and evaluate the metrics.
Monitor any changes in trends and algorithms.
Report on trend and algorithmic results.

Here is another example of a SOP diagram:

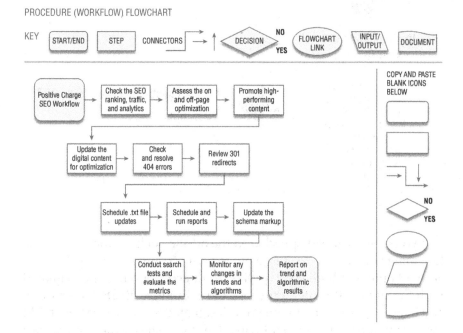

PROCEDURE (WORKFLOW) FLOWCHART

These are just sample templates; you can choose any template or format you want to outline the procedures and draft a diagram among your experts. Once it's complete, you're now ready for deployment.

Phase 6: Deploying and Going Live

Now that your SOPs are in place and your experts are onboarded, you're ready to deploy your MVP, functioning prototype, or POC.

Implementation & After Go-Live

This is where you take your preparation and begin implementing. You will spin it up, iterate, and validate if the outcomes pass your go/no-go criteria.

- MVP, Functioning Prototype, POC
- Iterations

If you haven't already purchased the off-the-shelf solution, that's the first thing you need to do. Reach out to your account rep or register your account online, submit your credit card or account number designated with the right cost center, purchase the solution, activate the account, and begin experimenting with your designated team. Notice how I said "experimenting" and not deploying. Once you start, expect to iterate a few times before you land on a final solution. This is very much expected.

Sometimes it's taken me four to six times with some use cases to finally figure out the software, specifically, its features, functionality, kinks, and how it weaves into the processes we outlined in prior phases. Sometimes because of the limitations of the software, or the feature we need doesn't get released for another quarter or two, we've had to adjust our processes temporarily to accommodate the current AI solution until it catches up to what we need.

We've even been stuck assuming the software does something it doesn't because we didn't ask up front and just assumed. So, it's important you work through all those kinks when evaluating the right software for you. Otherwise, you may be forced to switch solutions, which happens by the way, and you want to make sure you bake in ample time for that switch or surprise.

To summarize, for implementation, the steps after buying a solution are to activate the account, experiment, iterate, land on an outcome that passes your performance threshold after testing, and then deploy to production.

In the rare case you choose to pursue an off-the-model or off-the-LLM solution, you'll need to consider the following:

- Cloud versus on-prem options
- Framework for your algorithms (i.e. Pytorch)
- Big data processing platform (i.e. Spark)
- ETL for data pipelines
- Reporting
- Real-time processing needs (i.e. Kafka)
- And more

Lucky for you, you don't have to worry about any of that if you chose an off-the-shelf solution. Also, while you're iterating, communicate the progress back to the teams and iterate how AI will do the following:

- Amplify their work
- Accelerate current workloads
- Automate mundane and repetitive tasks

It may sound silly, but remember, you're the rogue executive who's asking and leading this organization into new ventures. It may be easy for you to understand the benefits of AI, and it may feel natural for you to experiment and bend the rules without breaking the spirit; however, not everyone is rogue at their core. Many, if not most, prefer predictable outcomes and consistency and will passively if not actively think, "Will my job be eliminated?" So, repeat the message until it sticks.

Key Outcomes

When all is said and done and you go live with your off-the-shelf solution, you should experience the following:

- Uncertainty but excitement because you're producing expected outcomes, and it wasn't as bad as you thought. That's partially due to all the preparation and anticipation up to deployment.
- You're generating the expected business value and distributing, communicating, and posting the results for public consumption. This is important because you want facts influencing people, not heresy perceptions.

■ You'll have identified people in your tribe who are natural born leaders, rogues, and change agents. This has happened in every one of my deployments. A natural byproduct of deploying AI is seeing who steps up to the plate and is willing to lead in uncertain times. You want those people around you.

■ You'll have clear business and product owners. The owners become somewhat obvious in the process because of both their interest and the depth at which they learn and absorb everything we've discussed in phases 3 and 4.

■ You'll have to assess your vendors, consultants, and temporary SMEs to see who you want to continue working with for your next and more advanced AI deployment.

■ You'll have involved cross-functional teams when needing the right support or subject-matter expertise, bringing even more visibility into your thought leadership and drive to change the status quo.

■ You'll have engaged the stakeholders and produced the results you promised. This is always great for your career.

■ You have a baseline measure of before and after improvements, which allows you to be data-driven in decision making versus feeling-driven. This makes it an objective conversation versus a subjective one.

■ You'll have a good basis for calculating total cost of ownership (TCO) and validating your business case whether it be efficiency, effectiveness, productivity, expert-based, or growth.

■ An unexpected but always good output is also you've documented your processes. You'll have a user guide and a "how-to" manual for anyone new who comes on board or any existing teammate who has questions about the process and how things are done.

Once you go live, it's important you don't forget your change management plan, communications plan, and project management plan outlined for this phase. You'll also need to set up town halls and office hours. Both are intended to be proactive about getting the pulse of the team, identifying potential areas for resistance, and soliciting feedback that isn't being publicly shared. This allows you to continually monitor the situation and get ahead of any situation before it sparks (which can happen).

Sad but true, but I once had a vice president who was intentionally trying to sabotage a project, but I wasn't aware until one month after we went live. Why? He was against it from the start because it required him to change his routine, learn new things, and set a new standard for performance for himself and his team. I found out about his plans and what he was secretly doing during office hours. Someone shared it with me in passing, and I was able to get ahead of it before he caused more damage.

Like I've said before, the technology isn't your biggest hurdle; the real project killers are your people. Let's get into that next.

Your Project Killers: The Wrong People

As you set off on your AI Journey, prepare to encounter a captivating array of individuals, and with them frustrations. Throughout my professional journey and after handling dozens of large-scale AI deployments, I've come to understand that the team you assemble and how you manage the personalities plays the most crucial role in determining your success, regardless of the project's size. As such, I want you to be well-acquainted with the personalities and resistance you may encounter when working with individuals who struggle to adapt to the changes AI will bring. More importantly, I will discuss how best to work with them. This chapter will discuss how to build a new team or work with an existing team you've inherited. I will also share a personal story of the most extreme case of people challenges I ever faced in all my years.

Change Ain't Easy

We all understand that change can be difficult, and for some, it can be even more challenging. With AI projects, there is no shortage of person-alities and a cast of characters that will be both supportive and resistant. Who could have anticipated that venturing into AI would bring forth both heroes and villains, while also uncovering surprising truths about yourself and your leadership style? It's akin to a business-themed super-hero movie, except without the capes!

> **NOTE**   Getting serious for a moment, none of the frameworks, principles, and tips that I have shared with you in the previous chapters prove effective if you are unaware of how to manage the personalities you will encounter when initiating your AI project, so pay close attention to this chapter.

The process of change management required to transition individuals, teams, and your organization from the current state to a desired state will be the most time-consuming and potentially frustrating aspect of deploying AI.

I was surprised too when I first started my AI journey. The sad thing is, you wouldn't know this fact unless you've had a few face plants under your belt.

> **NOTE**   Never underestimate your biggest project killer, the wrong people!

This is precisely why I have written this chapter and dedicated a whole chapter to it. The team you assemble or inherit plays the most crucial role in determining your success, regardless of the project's size.

Challenges are inevitable with AI; they are inherent to the work, not because of AI itself per se but because it's new to you and the organization. New things are always more challenging than the work we're familiar with. However, your ability to rebound and resolve these issues depends on the team you bring together. This is why it is vital for you to choose your team carefully. If you're in the situation where you don't have control over the individuals you onboard and you are just expected to work with many cross-functional teams, then at a minimum be prepared for what you may face.

Whether you are establishing a new team, taking over an existing one, or have the flexibility to select from an existing pool, this chapter will equip you with how to select and choose your team and effectively navigate the diverse personalities you will encounter. As such, we will discuss these areas:

Team Virtues   Here I outline what characteristics and traits you should look for when forming a team that has minimal to no experience in AI. I've also included a "will/skill matrix" so you know who to invest time in and who to let go.

The 10 AI Archetypes   The AI archetypes, much like the characters in *Snow White and the Seven Dwarfs*, are indeed real, and you will undoubtedly come across them. Throughout my experience, particularly when inheriting a sizable team rather than starting from scratch, I have consistently encountered these 10 archetypes. Now that I have experience, it takes me only a few weeks to identify who's who and to effectively collaborate with them. For you it might take a little longer, but you'll spot them so don't get discouraged! I've compiled the list of 10 for you and a "how-to" guide on navigating these personalities, which will significantly expedite your learning process.

Change Management Cheat Sheet   This will help you through your change management plan and help you plan and prepare proactively prior to starting your project.

Team Virtues

Countless leadership books have been written about building "high-performing" teams; this section is not that. Instead, it aims to provide a concise and straightforward approach to identifying the qualities in individuals who will maximize the chances of success for you and your AI project.

Throughout my experience, I have come to understand that, while technology, processes, and best practices can be taught, there are three virtues that cannot: grit, ambition, and resilience. These virtues, in my opinion, are the essential elements for constructing a winning team for your AI project.

> **NOTE**   High-performing teams aren't born but built. They require the raw ingredients, and in the case of AI projects, grit enables persistence, ambition fuels excellence, and resilience empowers one to overcome challenges.

As a business leader venturing into the world of AI or a practitioner trying to construct a team that consistently produces favorable outcomes, you need to do more than simply recruit exceptional talent. It involves pinpointing individuals who embody grit, ambition, and resilience: the three essential qualities for instigating transformation in any fresh endeavor you aspire to undertake.

Grit is unwavering determination that empowers an individual to persist through obstacles and sustain their efforts over a prolonged duration. It is crucial for navigating the inevitable highs and lows of new projects, such as the ones you'll encounter with AI.

Ambition is the relentless drive in a person for accomplishment and advancement. It is an innate force that propels us and our teams to constantly seek progress and refuse to settle for mediocrity.

Resilience is having someone who can swiftly recover from difficulties and adjust to change. It is what enables you and your team to bounce back from setbacks and remain agile in a dynamic market.

While people are inherently diverse with varying needs, if you have the authority to assemble a team for your initial AI project, prioritize these three virtues at all costs.

In addition to the virtues, it's also advantageous to assess the availability of talent using the will/skill matrix I've provided here. I can't claim credit for this matrix, and a simple search will yield a variety of versions; I have adapted this concept specifically for AI projects.

The quadrant below serves as a convenient tool to aid you in your decision-making process when it comes to hiring or onboarding teams.

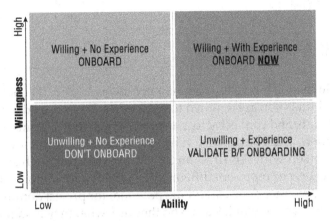

The Experienced and Willing   This is a no-brainer: onboard them quickly as they have a wealth of knowledge in various technology, AI, or business projects and are willing to endure the inevitable challenges. All of this will be an asset to you, your team, and the project. They are experienced and eager, which is the best combo.

The Inexperienced but Willing   Embrace these individuals despite their lack of experience as their determination and drive will be invaluable. Technology, processes, and best practices can be taught, but the innate desire to make an impact and explore new ventures is a rare quality, and they can be your trusty right hand with your AI projects.

The Unwilling with Experience   This group poses a challenge, as it requires time to discern whether their lack of motivation stems from laziness or other factors. If their lack of motivation is a result of external factors, they can potentially transition to the top-right quadrant with the right encouragement and environment. However, if their laziness (or apathy) is truly the cause, it is best to avoid engaging with them and move onto other options.

The Unwilling with No Experience   Run. Don't hesitate. Swiftly distance yourself from these folks as your project will end before it has even started.

In conclusion, when combining the three virtues of grit, ambition, and resilience with the quadrant of the willing and unwilling team members, it creates a strong foundation and basis for decision-making when forming your team. From here, you can feel confident that the team of individuals you've selected are committed to driving innovation and achieving success.

The 10 AI Archetypes

In certain leadership roles, you may not always have full control over the individuals you are required to work with. This can lead to the need to collaborate and connect across a variety of functions, teams, vendors, stakeholders, and consultants. When starting, it's important you familiarize yourself with the 10 AI archetypes to navigate such situations. These archetypes represent different personality types you are likely to encounter, their tendencies, and the potential for project derailment. As such, in this section you'll learn who they are, what they tend to do, and the most effective ways to collaborate with them to avoid any derailments of your project. The 10 archetypes are as follows:

- The Naysayer
- The Evangelist
- The Doer
- The Discerner
- The Blind
- The Curmudgeon
- The Saint
- The Optimist
- The Data Scientist
- The Know-It-All

First things first, prior to being able to identify who's who among the 10 archetypes, know this:

- Not everyone is cut out for strategic thinking.
- Not everyone has developed the muscle for critical thinking.
- Many like to disrupt conversations for the sake of disruption and provide no value through solutions.
- Some can't think big enough and lack the imagination of the "Art of the Possible."
- Some are driven by fear and worry about job security more than business value.

As the leader of the pack, you're going to have to monitor this closely and control who you spend time with, and how to manage meetings, so you're productive and as constructive as possible. This is of utmost importance, as neglecting to exercise discernment in these initial discussions can sabotage your project from the very beginning.

Filtering out the right participants for these conversations is the most significant action you can take to ensure a successful AI journey for yourself and your company. Much like family gatherings, where some members bring drama while others bring joy, the same dynamics can be expected here. In the following section, I will provide you with an overview of different personality types, their tendencies, their contributions, and the best approaches to manage them.

The Naysayer

This is probably the easiest group to identify. They have a tendency of saying "I don't think so" or "Yeah but" or "I don't think that will work." They are the dream killers of your AI project because they are quick to point out problems before solutions. They are easy to identify because they are typically not shy about sharing their point of view regardless of the impact it is having on the project and their teammates.

When it comes to their involvement, exclude them from your AI vision, mission, and strategy discussions and exclude them from your AI use-case selection process. Begin including them in some of the requirements sessions and incorporate them when reviewing both your design and solutions. Why? Their default reaction is to spot problems. As a result, they will automatically call out issues and poke holes in any assumptions, theories, or processes, and they will be a great litmus test for your thought process. This is vital because it'll give you the opportunity to uncover blind spots early on.

The Evangelist

The evangelist is the quarterback of your team and spreads good business energy to everyone.

This is the person you treat with care and bring alongside to every strategy, use case, and alignment discussion (assuming they can contribute substance). They refuse to use the word "no" and instead prioritize the word "how" and focus their efforts on finding solutions. They maintain their drive even when tired and are always ready to take on any challenges. They keep the team momentum going when fatigue sets in and are up for any challenge.

When it comes to their involvement, include them in your AI vision, mission, and strategy discussions and your AI use case discussions. Include them in your design discussions, but be selective about when you need them for detailed design and/or solution discussions. The details can zap the energy of an evangelist, and protecting their energy levels is your priority.

Limit their involvement in detailed status updates, and pull them in only when the team requires their guidance and decision-making skills in strategic conversations. This approach is necessary to ensure you conserve their energy, enabling them to contribute their full potential.

The Doer

This group is the backbone of your team. They show up consistently, embrace responsibility, and stay accountable for their work and their actions, at all costs. They deliver results without needing oversight and are often the silent engine that drives your business forward. They are critical to the success of your AI project.

When it comes to their involvement, exclude them from your AI strategy and use-case discussions; that's too high level for them. However, include them in your design discussions as they will need context to do their work. Include them when discussing business and technical requirements and solutions. They love details and will shine in this phase of the work. They also like to be at the center of it all, so keep them engaged in the decision-making process; it's inherently important to them. Make sure to celebrate their milestones and acknowledge their work. While this group tends to be quiet, they secretly like to be thanked. So, acknowledge their work through the project. It drives them to do what they do for you.

The Discerner

These individuals are always inquisitive and tend to operate at a higher level. They possess a desire to comprehend the underlying reasons and objectives behind your thoughts and ideas. They possess a keen intuition that allows them to differentiate between well-developed ideas and those that are merely a fleeting thought. At first glance, one may mistake them for naysayers, but discerners are distinct individuals with genuine interest in making sure ideas are thoroughly considered before implementation. They have the best interests of the team at heart. Yet dealing with them can be exhausting due to their incessant questioning, and there will be moments when your team becomes frustrated with them.

When it comes to their involvement, include them in your AI vision, mission, and strategy discussions. They will flush out the details with you and make sure you're thinking through your "why" and the direction of everything. Also include them in your AI use-case discussions, as they will ensure all ideas are thoroughly considered. Be selective about when you include them in design discussions and status meetings because you don't want them hindering progress with more questions. It's best to exclude them from solutioning, deep dives, and the deployment process.

The Blind

This is the person who is completely oblivious to the situation at hand; they show up to meetings, rarely participate, appear disengaged, and typically multitask because none of your words or actions captivates their interest. They simply don't care about the project because it's another "shiny toy" project causing people to react.

If you can avoid this type of individual in your project, I strongly suggest you do so. It will only consume your time and energy. However, if you must involve them, extend an invitation to attend meetings as optional, but refrain from expecting any contribution or assigning them tasks.

The Curmudgeon

The curmudgeon has a tendency to be irritable, is overly critical, and isn't a fan of new ideas or ways of doing things. They tend to be sharp-tongued, not well liked by team members, and can dampen team morale quickly. Like the blind, if you don't have to include them, don't. The curmudgeon's personality goes against the very nature of transformational or exploratory projects.

When it comes to their involvement, exclude them from your AI vision, mission, use-case selection, and design discussions. Yet include them in business and technical requirement and solutions discussions, but only to review the work once done, not to brainstorm or establish the requirements. Sometimes their experience and seasoned exposure can shed light into an opportunity, and their cautious outlook can be a good stress test for requirements and solutions.

The Saint

The saint in your team is an empath, the individual who can pick up on subtle cues such as a teammates' unspoken stress or the collective mood in a room. They are often the first to reach out to a co-worker who is struggling. Saints are invaluable during times of change or conflict as they can provide insight into various perspectives and mediate with a sense of fairness. This individual is key to your project's morale and to connecting individual goals into a collective objective.

When it comes to their involvement, attendance for them is optional in your AI vision, mission, strategy, use-case selection, and design discussions (it depends on their ability to contribute to strategic thinking). Yet, absolutely include them in your status meetings so they can observe the healthy (or unhealthy) debates and tensions that are slowly becoming under currents. Also include them in all deep dives because this is where conflict and stress tend to arise and where they can help the most.

The Optimist

The optimist is usually always positive, has a tendency of nodding and agreeing whenever someone says something, plays neutral, and rarely has a distinct point of view themselves. While it's good to be around optimists, for AI projects, they rarely contribute anything of value. Since your goal is to craft pods of contributors, be selective about when to bring this person into the conversation. Keep your teams small and actionable.

When it comes to their involvement, exclude them from your AI vision, mission, strategy, and use-case selection discussions; they likely won't provide much value there. Attendance is optional in design discussions, status meetings, solutioning, deep dive, and deployment.

The Data Scientist

The data scientist (or the hard-core technologist) in your team is a critical teammate, as they likely possess the technical knowledge you may need, or at minimum, they can understand the new space and all the jargon that goes with it. Data scientists have all sorts of styles from open-minded and collaborative to being laser-focused on the solution without being concerned about the business value. They sometimes struggle with timelines and budgets, get lost in the research, and might not connect the work back to your "why" as you would like. However, this person's technical knowledge will be super helpful to you and will be needed on the project; just don't give them more weight than others.

When it comes to their involvement, if they are open-minded, collaborative, and receptive to learning the business value and the "why," include them starting from the design phase. If, however, they go off on tangents, have a tendency to focus on the solution, and can't really relate to the team and the work that's been put in so far, include them in solutioning and deployment phases only. Monitor the discussions and see if you're able to keep the meeting on track with their involvement. Step in immediately if you feel this person is taking the team away from the main priority. Make sure your project manager and/or lead is very clear on timelines and deliverables with them.

The Know-It-All

The "know-it-all" has a tendency of thinking they have superior knowledge on every subject, regardless of the context or the expertise of others around them. They tend to dominate the conversation, disregard expertise, offer unsolicited advice, boast about their knowledge and, worse, resist learning. Therefore, it's important you contain this archetype to protect the rest of the team.

Exclude them from your AI vision, mission, strategy, and use-case selection discussions. Make it optional for them to attend the design and requirements phase. Include them in solutioning since they can sometimes provide a unique point of view that's worth listening too, and by then, the team hasn't reached fatigue with their anecdotes, so they will be more apt to listening.

In summary, spotting the personality types across the 10 AI archetypes is key to knowing who's who in your AI team, how to best work with them, and how to leverage their personalities in the best way possible. The goal is really to help you jump-start your project and make sure your team doesn't become the silent killer. By knowing the personalities, it helps level-set expectations so you can collaborate more effectively, anticipate contributions, and make the most of unique characteristics, without having to learn on the job and manage your frustrations daily.

Change Management

Understanding the personalities of AI is just one aspect of managing a successful team in your AI deployment. Change management is also a crucial factor in ensuring that AI is integrated smoothly into an organization.

Throughout my experience in deploying transformational programs and/or AI projects, I have yet to witness change management executed effectively. It's sad but true. The reason why are as follows:

Unclear Ownership   Who is responsible for change management? Is it HR? An external vendor? Internal stakeholders? You? The situation becomes even more chaotic when the answer is "all of the above," as there is no clarity in ownership resulting in overlapping responsibilities and a fast-paced mess.

Insufficient Investments   Change management always falls victim to insufficient investments. Despite acknowledging its importance and emphasizing its value, very few resources are allocated to executing on the initial plans. We may discuss it and recognize its significance, but when it comes to planning the program and allocating budgets, change management is often overlooked.

Definition   It also doesn't help that the meaning of change management varies for everyone. We fail to establish clear definitions and roles for it within programs, leaving people to make assumptions. And since change management is directly tied to culture, defining what it is is even more critical because the bigger the company, the tougher it is to shift its culture.

Furthermore, teams often use the term as a broad, all-encompassing phrase to discuss general people-related issues. Change management is so much more, and throughout my years of experience in implementing AI projects, I have acquired extensive knowledge in navigating change management. In this section, I have condensed the knowledge into an "Essentials List" for your convenience.

You can read and research a more formal structure for your change management program (there are countless books out there) should you desire to go deeper in this field. However, the "Essentials List" I provide here is a top 10 list of what I have observed are critical to AI projects:

Manifesto   Craft a concise manifesto that clearly outlines the vision, mission, and rationale behind the "why" of the transformation, and don't stop repeating the "why." You can never over emphasize your purpose. Consistently incorporate it into every meeting, document, and conversation to make it stick and resonate.

Leadership Alignment   Ensure you have leadership alignment so that no one is undermining or passively resisting behind the scenes. Don't assume you have alignment; really make sure you have active activism and not passive support. The best way to do that is through office hours and town halls with anonymous Q&A. You'll quickly become familiar with the undercurrents of sentiment.

Transition   Spend some time and think through your transition plan. How are you going to transition individuals, business processes, and the technology while maintaining business continuity and not interrupting your operations?

Communication   Think through how to establish and effectively communicate the anticipated changes in the ways of working. What measures will you take to maintain transparency and effectively communicate the impact on jobs, expectations, and the need for urgency? Any written or verbal format is acceptable as long as its frequent and consistent.

Involvement   Involve your employees in the change process. Enlist the support of your advocates, evangelists, saints, and optimists, and meet with them regularly and have them spread the good word and the "why."

Small Victories   Establish a plan to celebrate small victories so that fatigue doesn't set prematurely.

Iteration   Make it clear that immediate results should not be expected and that sufficient time is needed for change to take root, as not to undermine the transformation efforts. Articulate that this is not a simple switch that can be flipped on, yielding immediate and visible results. It will take time to iron out the details and realize the value.

Monitoring   Continuously monitor progress, team morale, and impact so that you can openly guide your team through the advancements and proactively adjust strategies.

Retrospectives   Retrospectives are key to have with your leadership team monthly, if not more frequently. Retrospectives keep everyone aligned with the progress, issues, and risks. Some feel they're beneficial only for the project team, but I have learned that they are beneficial for stakeholders as they ensure alignment and accountability. And for any items that need immediate course correction, the leadership team is involved.

Changes   Make changes when needed, be transparent about them, and communicate the "why." It shows your seriousness and focus to AI and sets the tone and stage for expectations. If changes are needed, align, decide, and act.

This is the condensed top 10 list, for your convenience. Feel free to utilize any medium you prefer: emails, PowerPoint presentations, Word documents, town halls, team meetings, or newsletters. Don't get caught up in overthinking the process, because the format in which you communicate is less important than taking the initiative to do so consistently.

Now, a tale of caution: despite the guidance provided about building a successful team, understanding the 10 AI archetypes, and implementing effective change management strategies, it's important to acknowledge that sometimes not everything will go according to plan. Life has a way of throwing unexpected challenges our way; it's called Murphy's law. In those moments, your leadership skills will be put to the test. I'm not exaggerating.

To demonstrate, I'd like to share a real story with you that tested my patience, resilience, IQ, EQ, BQ, and SQ. This is a story where the rogue executive in me was ready to quit; my team of gritty, ambitious, and resilience teammates were ready to throw the towel and despite the fact that we did most of the things I outlined previously, we learned new things because of the extreme challenges that we faced. I share this story only because I want you to be prepared for the extreme cases, while preparing you for how a majority of projects will go.

The Dumpster Fire

I was brought on board to transform a companies data, analytics, and AI capabilities. It's a task that now feels effortless to me, but never in my life had I faced so many obstacles. Here's how it started.

Before I joined the company and during the interview process, I inquired about the company's experience with hiring leaders in my space. What were some of capabilities and accomplishments in place? What skills were needed to acclimate to the existing company culture? Had they hired prior executives to lead the space? These were all normal interview questions. Unfortunately for me, they weren't entirely transparent with their responses. It wasn't until I joined the company that I found out there were two previous leaders, both had been fired or asked to leave.

What I was told was, both leaders struggled with the culture and were deemed ineffective. While it was not uncommon for one leader to face difficulties, it was unusual for two to struggle for the same reasons. However, I pushed forward not thinking much of it because the very things that the former leaders found challenging happened to be my strengths. I had endured so much hazing in my personal and professional life that I was numb to obstacles. Additionally, I had successfully led major transformational projects in the past, so I approached this situation with confidence.

As time passed, I clearly knew what we needed to do for the company. I dedicated time to engage with business units and departments. I shared my ideas, got alignment, crafted the vision, mission, and strategy for us to evolve and advance our data, analytics, and AI agenda. I created a plan outlining the capabilities we intended to develop, along with the expected return on investment, growth, and margin gains. To support these plans, I also crafted a talent map and utilization plan for all team members. In my world, this was a straightforward executive deck, and I knew how to tell it well. The execs at the company were impressed, and I had no issues getting the funding I needed to get started.

As we mobilized on our plan, we initiated the first phase of projects, beginning with an automated intelligence project within the enterprise data management team. The goal of this project was to automate repetitive tasks, allowing resources to be allocated to more pressing business needs. Again, this seemed straightforward to me. It was a simple automation project. What could go wrong?

My team consisted of more than 150 individuals who were solely focused on enterprise data management, accounting for 35% of my overall team. Given my background at IBM and my expertise in MDM, I felt confident in my ability to understand and connect with this team. However, I soon realized, this would not be as straightforward as I had anticipated.

To begin, I started asking my leaders various questions. Unfortunately, they either didn't have the answers or deferred to someone else. I found this rather perplexing. In an attempt to gather more information, I inquired about the brands we served, the types of requests we received, and the systems and applications we utilized for our tasks. However, my leaders either ignored my questions or provided vague responses. The desire to make a good impression on the new boss was obviously not their priority.

After two unproductive months, I decided to alter my approach and seek answers directly from their leaders who they referenced as their experts time and time again. Then one day, I was called to HR. I discovered that my leadership team, the very same people who were unable to answer my questions or claimed they needed to consult their team, had filed a complaint regarding my circumvention. They felt I was going over their head. The news left me astounded. At first, I thought it was a joke. Was such behavior truly permissible? Was HR really entertaining this?

Now for context, on numerous occasions I was told by many that my "team" was difficult to work with, and it was unclear as to what they really did. Not only that, but the team was large and expensive. The "team" was always busy, always at capacity, and not able to take on any more work unless we hired more people.

I had shared this context with HR and recounted the events to them, including how many meetings, with whom, and the documented responses. After a few meetings, HR decided it was best to involve the vice presidents in future meetings to put this to rest. However, after another unproductive two months, I realized something wasn't right, and the entire team was in on something. So, I had to change tactics again since my own team seemed to be actively hindering any progress.

Determined to find a solution, I proactively reached out to the HR department. I explained the challenges I was facing and outlined my plan to address them through a big, bold, and comprehensive program called "Day in the Life." This program was aimed to unite my fragmented teams and foster a stronger sense of cohesion, ultimately enhancing our teams' collective capabilities and integrating our efforts across the data and analytics value chain. My hope was that we would all improve communication and learn how to better work with each other.

But for me, the goal of hosting this program was to shed light on what it was my "difficult" team was actually doing and why they were being so secretive. It was the only way I knew how to avoid singling them out and make it "HR friendly" while adding pressure on them. I was meticulous in crafting the program's messaging and purpose, recognizing the strategic maneuvering required in the delicate situation.

Luckily it worked. After 6 months of deliberation, I learned my team of 150+ was one massive copy-and-paste factory! Nearly all of their work was manual in nature, and a majority of my teammates had been with the company for more than 15 years. I was dealing with a tenured workforce, and job security was their number-one motive.

They were not going to let some new, hot-shot executive who had been with the company for six months disrupt their lives.

Unfortunately for them, I was well-acquainted with their space, and I was fully aware that their current level of productivity fell short of what was considered standard output. I knew what fair, good, and great looked like, and we were falling short on all three. Their output should have been six times more than what they were doing. As a result, I formulated a well-documented proposal on automation, highlighting the return on investment, our yields, and the additional work we would be able to take on.

The decision to pursue this course of action was undeniably in the best interest of the company, and the business units were in violent support. Best of all, we weren't laying off anyone. Instead, the team would take on additional scope of work that the business had been requesting for several years, without adding head count.

To ensure a smooth kick-off and transition plan, I meticulously devised a change management plan and set clear expectations for all stakeholders. I mentally prepared myself for challenges and obstacles, equipping myself with a well-thought-out strategy. Despite my belief that I had taken care of all necessary precautions, I soon discovered an entirely new set of issues.

Here's what quickly transpired:

- I learned the team had purposely not documented anything and relied solely on their tribal and institutional knowledge as a form of job security.

- They were not openly sharing how they performed their jobs, tasks, and workflows with the vendor we hired to help with automation. We can't automate if we don't know the work that needs to be automated.

- The team took extended vacations and PTOs to purposely slow everything down, hoping to hinder our ability to deliver on time and on budget.

- The vendor we hired had an intervention with us; they told us they were dropping us as a client because their teammates were being treated horribly by my teammates. I was mortified and had to address that quickly.

- I also learned the two prior leaders had quit because of this team. I know this because I reached out to both on LinkedIn to see what had happened and why they left. Both were open as a book and shared all the same challenges I was facing.

This project, which had clear ROI and value for the business, had turned into a dumpster fire for me. It gave me massive stress and massive heartburn, with little to no help from HR, my boss, and stakeholders. Why?

A group of people refused to change, and corporate culture was enabling this behavior. Comfort and complacency had kicked in, and the team did not want to change.

It also became evident that they knew if they held steadfast, they would outlast any new leader who came into the picture. After all, it had worked with the former leaders; it should work with me.

Unfortunately for them, they hadn't taken the time to get to know me, my past, and my level of grit, ambition, resilience, and rogue executive-ness. The "we will wait you out" game wasn't going to work on me, because I wasn't going anywhere. This rogue executive knew a thing or two about roadblocks and pushing past challenges. They weren't going to shake me down.

Long story short, we finished the project, we delivered what we needed, and we went through hell doing it. All this is to say, sometimes even with all the planning and experience in the world, some things may just fall apart! You'll second-guess yourself, you'll ask if it's worth it, you'll think about stopping mid-journey, or you may simply resign from the idea that you have a chance in hell to be successful. Just know that you're not alone, and it may happen. But what doesn't kill you makes you stronger.

Also, this was a very extreme case I shared with you, and it was intended only to paint a realistic picture of what extreme projects look like. Most AI projects are far from being this difficult, I promise! So, be hopeful, optimistic, and excited about your journey ahead.

Human in the Loop

In this chapter, we'll continue the discussion of how humans are critical to your AI projects but through a different lens. It's no longer about how to form a team or deal with difficult personalities but how humans are critical checkpoints in the AI process itself, regardless of what processes or tasks are being automated, augmented, or outsourced.

- We will discuss some of the legal and regulatory work that's taking place to make sure we incorporate AI in an ethical and governed way, and we'll discuss the four (4) layers of responsibility that go with it.

- We will discuss the six (6) tenets of responsible AI and the risks associated with AI that largely stem from unintended consequences that arise when good intentions go awry.

- We will discuss a concept called "human in the loop" that you need to incorporate into your deployments.

- I will share a personal story that occurred in December 2023 to cement the concept of "human in the loop."

What is "Human in the Loop"

Human in the loop refers to a framework within AI deployments where human judgment is incorporated into the AI decision-making process. It's a must-have process in any deployment.

This may sound boring, but this will be an entertaining chapter once you get to the story I share with you, because it's a doozy. But before we get into a story about "AI gone wrong" that involved me, I think it's only fair I give you a general understanding of what "human in the loop" means and its connection to *responsible AI*, a term you're hearing in the news, especially with all the AI acts and legislation being discussed globally.

Essentially, "human in the loop" ensures that your AI systems don't operate in a vacuum or give incorrect information to your employees or clients. It also ensures that the discerning eye of a human for values, ethics, and context is considered so AI systems align with human norms. The greatest value, however, is that it provides an extra pair of eyes to make sure we catch issues and whoopsies before anyone else does.

> **NOTE**   "Human in the loop" is intrinsically connected to the movement toward responsible AI, which advocates for the use of AI in an ethical, governed, and accountable way at a global scale.

"Human in the loop" is a necessary step for us as individuals when deploying AI, and responsible AI aims to address issues such as bias, fairness, and the potential negative societal impacts of AI.

Responsible AI

The term *Responsible AI* is an umbrella term that's being used broadly across a variety of media channels, articles, and academic publications. I personally think the term is being overused and we're not doing a great job of defining what it actually means to the public, but let me try and help with that.

What the term *Responsible AI* is intending to communicate is the approach we should take to developing and deploying AI systems in an ethical and legal way. The goals are ultimately safety and trustworthiness in all applications of AI by increasing transparency and reducing issues. But as we'll learn in the upcoming section, it's not that simple. As such, the movement of responsible AI is intended to put in guardrails so that AI applications have good intentions to empower employees, accelerate businesses, and impact customers in a good way.

> **NOTE** The dangers of AI largely arise from unintended consequences and good intentions going awry.

For now, just know there is a lot of pressure on companies such as OpenAI, Anthropic, Hugging Face, Amazon, and Google to have sound and responsible AI practices in place since they hold the keys to the kingdom right now. There's a mandate being established for these large companies who are powering both enterprises and AI-based companies to have clear, documented principles for operationalizing responsible AI, which include fairness, reliability, safety, privacy, security, inclusiveness, transparency, and accountability. It's easier said than done, though!

> **NOTE** Personal point of view and individual interpretation get in the way of deeming something to be "fair" or "sound." What's "fair" to you may not be "fair to me making the topic of Responsible AI a tricky one."

That's why definitions and interpretations get tricky. We see this in everyday business interactions, contract negotiations, and project decisions between teams. That's why governments are struggling to define what Responsible AI should mean, how to best scale the practices, and develop a manuscript or manifesto on what needs to be done. Furthermore, critical values such as anonymity, confidentiality, and controls can be interpreted in a variety of ways. That's why the goal of writing a clear, decisive, black-and-white manual that says, "you must do this" is nearly impossible to create for AI.

So, at this moment in time and in history, the objectives of Responsible AI are mostly focused on creating awareness, with guidelines to make sure companies small and large that choose to create or adopt AI capabilities implement sound and fair practices for their employees and customers. It's just the responsible thing to do (pun intended).

The Four (4) Layers of Responsibility

Just like not all AI is created equal, neither are the layers within the Responsible AI umbrella. What do I mean by this? Well, to uncomplicate a complicated concept, I've divided responsible AI into four (4) layers of responsibility.

- Governments
- The Enterprise
- Businesses
- Individuals

This may not be an overly inclusive list and I know for a fact we can divide and subdivide responsibilities further, but I'm choosing the four main layers to simplify things.

Governments

These are entities that reside at a federal, state, or local level that are comprised of departments, units, subdivisions, boards, bureaus, and commissions whose sole purpose is to protect the interest of the people and ensure we have order among society through laws and mandates. The government's role in Responsible AI is important because they are the only governing entity that can keep large tech companies in check. Without the government involved, we're at the mercy of what is being created by the big tech companies and their interpretation of "fair" and "just."

While we all know government entities are struggling to catch up with the progress of AI and how to best govern the developments and applications, we're at least making some progress. For example, the EU AI Act and the Canada Data and AI Act outline regulations for AI systems and impose penalties for noncompliance. While they are both still in early stages and we can expect iterations on the draft, I'm personally happy to see the discussions are happening. I won't go into the details of the acts in this book, because honestly, by the time you read this, a few more iterations will have been released and the content would be outdated.

The key here is to know governments are focused on Responsible AI so that it's not a free-for-all. The only critique I would have is they need to move faster. For the sake of proper AI governance, government entities need to get out of their own way, remove layers of bureaucracy, and get to the controls and mandates in place faster; otherwise, we may have a case where the kids in a daycare are self-governing themselves.

The Enterprise

This refers to organizations and businesses that are involved in the development, deployment, and use of AI systems and applications.

For both large tech companies and enterprises that reside across industries I later outline for us, they have a role in ensuring development and deployments are done with good intentions, empowering employees, and customers in the best way possible. Enterprises have a responsibility for implementing ethical AI practices to adhere to the fundamental criteria of soundness, fairness, transparency, accountability, and privacy while the government discusses how to best define these broad brushstroke terms.

Whether the aim is advanced research or leveraging tooling innovations at scale, everyone involved must put in place guidelines, standards, and ethical requirements to ensure enterprises meet legal requirements while mitigating legal risk. This is no longer the job of the compliance department or your lawyer. The enterprise as a whole now has a responsibility.

Businesses

This refers to companies that are typically privately owned corporations, partnerships, or sole proprietorships that have fewer employees and/or less annual revenue than the enterprise we identify with and are looking to adopt AI in some parts of their business to create greater efficiency or productivity.

> **NOTE** I think this is the sweet spot for AI application. There's so much efficiency to be gained, productivity to be amplified, and better service to be provided.

One of the reasons why I wrote this book is because I find so much fulfillment in seeing businesses thrive by integrating AI into their processes. It's not the easiest of career choices for sure, because businesses often think AI doesn't apply to their operations; but when I show them how, their eyes light up, and this is where we "deployers" and thought leaders create the most impact.

Businesses who apply AI are responsible for educating themselves on the best ways to deploy AI to get the business benefits they want while understanding the risks and limitations; holding the companies that built the off-the-shelf solution accountable, reporting any shady practices or things that can be interpreted as "unfair" or "unjust;" and, where possible, staying informed with regulations and collaborating with local programs.

Individuals

This refers to you, me, family members, friends, and society as a whole. As new tools and innovations are available to us, this fourth group has the largest responsibility of all. The companies that create the innovations wouldn't exist if not for us consumers who buy their innovations. We have the largest impact and the largest voice in defining what's "fair" and "just." Through our social media channels and platforms, we can absolutely impact which companies survive and which don't. As a matter of fact, it was because of us that advocacy for data privacy and transparency regulations forced the topic of General Data Protection Regulation (GDPR) and now Responsible AI. Our voice matters, regardless of our technical expertise when we apply common sense and critical thinking to ensure AI applications are safe and fair.

The four layers of responsibility were laid out to demonstrate the impact we all have on the future of how AI is designed and treated. While it may seem like a distant or foreign concept right now, it's not. We all have influence as to how this technology advances.

The Six (6) Tenets of Responsible AI

Within the context of Responsible AI, we have explored the different layers of responsibility and the overarching objective of promoting fairness and justice in the implementation of AI in various settings. However, we have yet to delve into is the specific principles of Responsible AI and the challenges and varying interpretations that come with them.

The risks associated with AI largely stem from unintended consequences that arise when good intentions go awry. Therefore, the six principles outlined aim to raise awareness about the potential hazards that can arise from the use or misuse of algorithms. We will also come to understand that not everything is straightforward. I provide examples for each of the six key principles and the accompanying examples that spark intense discussions on how to approach Responsible AI and establish effective governance.

Transparency

Transparency entails clear communication about how AI systems are being used to build trust. It plays a major role in data privacy and governance, requiring companies to expose their data collection practices and intended uses.

Sounds simple. However, in May 2023, CNET management got into some hot water with its employees when management decided to leverage AI for content creation. As a matter of fact, it got CNET, BuzzFeed, and

Sports Illustrated into some trouble because employees were wanting transparency into the use and process.

Well, one can argue that management should absolutely be transparent about its intended use of AI in content creation. But on the other hand, you have employees and union workers saying, "In this time of instability, our diverse content teams need industry-standard job protections, fair compensation, editorial independence, and a voice in the decision-making process, especially as automated technology threatens our jobs and reputations."

As such, transparency is key, but not for the purpose of job security. Employees are coming from a place of fear and want job stability so they resist change. While transparency is crucial and a fundamental right, what makes it complicated is situational context. Sure, establishing boundaries that respect employee freedom is key, but so is preserving the longevity of the company and its ability to adapt to new standards and ways of working.

Accountability

Accountability is about having mechanisms in place to address any issues or harm that AI systems may cause and having accountability into those outcomes. This area is especially tricky because it requires us to clearly define the division of labor, roles, and responsibilities, and establish new laws to hold the involved parties accountable. As we see from the following example, that gets tricky.

The year 2018 marked the death of Elaine Herzberg, the first recorded case of a pedestrian fatality involving a self-driving car. During a test-drive conducted by Uber, one of their autonomous vehicles collided with Elaine as she was jaywalking across a four-lane road in Arizona at night. Several factors contributed to this tragic accident.

- First, the software utilized by the self-driving car was unable to identify jaywalkers, leading to the question of whether it should have accounted for illegal actions performed by humans.

- Second, despite the presence of a safety driver in the vehicle during the test, that person was unable to react in time to prevent the collision. This raises the issue of their responsibility in such a situation. They were the safeguard after all.

- Third, there was a debate regarding the adequacy of street lighting during the nighttime incident and whether both the car and the safety driver could have spotted the jaywalker and avoided the accident if the streets were well light. This brings into question the potential liability of the city.

▪ Last, it is worth considering that Elaine was engaging in the illegal act of jaywalking, which is typically classified as an infraction or misdemeanor. Thus, it can be debated whether she should bear the consequences of her actions, especially considering the late hour at which the illegal act occurred.

So, who's ultimately accountable in the case of Elaine? Uber, the city, the safety driver, or Elaine? As you can see, the answer isn't always as clean as we think.

Fairness

Fairness means AI models and algorithms should be free from biases that can lead to discrimination against certain groups, providing equal opportunities for all users. The tricky part about fairness is that our society is polarized, and there is bias with all the news outlets, media, and social channels. Therefore, teaching a machine to be unbiased is difficult when our data is inherently biased and the same data we use to train the machines.

For example, Meta's business model and algorithms allow advertisers to target specific groups, which means they have the ability to exclude specific groups when trying to up-sell and cross-sell products and services that don't meet the advertisers' requirements. One could argue that targeted advertising is not only effective in consumer outreach but also cost-effective for the advertiser. It allows advertisers to micro-target and reach niche audiences, such as swing-state voters concerned about climate change. However, on the flip side, and part of the selection process, you can de-select groups, which means you can de-select certain races, socio-economic statuses, age groups, and more. Does that mean Meta is now encouraging and enabling bias in their models? One would think not, as Meta says its policies prohibit advertisers from using the targeting options for discrimination, harassment, or disparagement. However, the question is, if the options exist due to the data collected by Meta, will people naturally be inclined to practice bias?

Privacy

The tenet of privacy is about protecting sensitive data and respecting user consent. All existing data privacy laws like CCPA, COPA, and

GDPR must be upheld, with additional layers and laws applied due to AI. That makes sense, right? Well, not so fast. We as a society have all but relinquished our rights to data privacy when we consent, opt in, and accept the terms and conditions of all the apps we use on our phone and desktop. In essence, we're allowing companies to use our data, sell our data, and re-purpose our data in exchange for the conveniences of the apps we use.

In the year 2022, Clearview AI, a facial recognition company, claimed to be on track to amass 100 billion facial photos in its database within a year. They proudly stated that they already had 14 photos of each of the 7 billion people on Earth, essentially making everyone identifiable. Their objective is to support a surveillance system that can be utilized by numerous law enforcement and government agencies worldwide for arrests and criminal investigations. While some may argue that this will contribute to safer communities, others believe that it infringes upon our privacy rights. Certain cities and states have implemented bans or restrictions on facial recognition technology, while countries like China and England consistently employ it for criminal identification. The question at hand is to what degree should Clearview AI respect privacy rights when we have willingly consented to the use of our data and have shared our images of ourselves, our friends, and family members on social media? As you can see, there could be endless points of view on the topic of privacy.

Inclusiveness

Inclusiveness represents the need for AI to be accessible to diverse populations, respecting and embracing differences. No community, company, or collection of groups should be excluded from leveraging AI if they so choose. This sounds obvious, but with the great "digital divide" of the haves and have-nots, is inclusiveness achievable? I have recently gotten involved with a few organizations to try to reduce the digital divide but the problem is pervasive in rural areas, between the educated and the uneducated, between socioeconomic groups, and globally, between the more and less industrially developing countries. It affects all aspects of life, including education, employment, healthcare, and civic engagement. While I'm glad inclusiveness is included in the tenets of Responsible AI, there's a larger and more fundamental issue at hand in the great digital divide. Developing countries are still struggling to get clean water, so I'm not sure access to AI is their number-one priority, but I guess it's good to highlight as a fifth tenet.

Diversity and Nondiscrimination

The tenet of diversity and nondiscrimination involves reducing biases in AI algorithms, using diverse and representative datasets, and ensuring that AI systems do not perpetuate or amplify discriminatory practices. By upholding the values of diversity and nondiscrimination, organizations can mitigate the risks of biases and discrimination in AI model decisions, creating a more inclusive and equitable environment.

Sounds simple, right? It's not. In 2019, a Diversity & Non-Discrimination Act in AI was violated in an algorithm in the U.S. healthcare system that demonstrated racial bias unintentionally. The algorithm was developed by a well-established data and analytics company known as Optum. The algorithm was intended to help hospitals and insurance companies identify which patients would benefit from "high-risk care management" programs. The programs were aimed to preemptively stave off serious health complications, ultimately reducing costs and the burden on the healthcare system. What they found instead was the algorithm was underestimating the needs of the sickest Black patients, leading to denied access to the program. The algorithm wasn't intentionally racist; in fact, it specifically excluded race as a distinction marker. However, the dataset used to train the model showed that Black patients incurred about $1,800 less in medical costs per year than white patients with the same number of chronic conditions; thus, the algorithm scored white patients as more at risk of future health problems than Black patients, simply due to cost factors, which the program intended to fix. Therefore, white patients were recommended into the program more than Black patients since it was targeting the group more at risk. For all intents and purposes, the intent was good, the model was sound, and the data was right, but yet, the question of discrimination was brought up, and Optum had to shut down the model supporting the program, slowing the progress of the intended use of the program.

Human in the Loop

Now that we have a strong grasp of what Responsible AI is and the roles, responsibilities, and complexities associated with putting in place global and macro measures to keep development and deployments of AI "fair" and "just," let's circle back to "human in the loop."

Earlier I mentioned that this was a must-have process in any deployment. Seriously. If there's anything you take away from this chapter, it's that you need someone on your team overseeing the outcomes of your AI application to make sure it aligns with your businesses practices and the outputs you want.

I've been in countless situations where I'm advising clients on how to deploy AI, and I emphasize the review process by asking, "Who on your team is going to review the outputs of the AI solution before it's sent to a client or triggers a business process within your organization?" I usually get a blank stare.

In addition to these tasks:

- Choosing the right AI strategy
- Selecting the right use case
- Picking the right team
- Being prepared to deal with the different AI archetypes

ensuring you have a "human in the loop" is the next most critical step. Make sure you have real people checking the work and validating its appropriateness before anything is distributed.

Why do I feel so bullish about this topic? It's because I was personally the victim of an AI solution gone wrong when a company decided to skip the "human in the loop" process in December 2023. Here's a personal story of what happens when you skip having a "human in the loop."

My Nightmare

What they say is right: "Common sense isn't so common." Sadly.

I woke up one Monday morning, December 18, 2023, around 5 a.m.; I fed the cat, made my coffee, and sat in my corner chair to read, write, and catch up on news. It was a typical weekday morning for me.

Around 5:30 a.m., I got an alert about an article that was posted on Google with my name on it. I clicked the link and read "The Husband of Sol Rashidi: Unveiling the Man Behind the Name." The subtitle read "Uncovering the enigmatic figure behind Sol Rashidi as we delve into the life and identity of her husband in this captivating and revealing article."

Ummm. . .what? What is this? I continued reading.

The opening paragraph in this 8-page article read "In order to truly understand the success of Sol Rashidi, one must delve into the man who has been her steadfast partner throughout her journey. While Sol's name has become synonymous with achievement and innovation, her husband has played a crucial role in supporting and empowering her along the way."

Again, what? While technically my husband has been of tremendous support and over the past few years he's taken on the lion's share of school drop-offs and pick-ups for our two young children, something about the article, its intent, still seemed off. I continued to read.

This article aims to shed light on the personal and professional life of the man behind the name, providing insight into their shared values, mutual support, and the impact he has had on Sol's remarkable success.

In addition to his intellectual pursuits, he also finds solace in nature. He enjoys spending time outdoors, whether it's hiking through lush forests, strolling along sandy beaches, or simply basking in the beauty of a picturesque sunset. The tranquility of nature rejuvenates his spirit and allows him to find peace amidst the chaos of everyday life.

They clearly don't know my husband. . .but I continue reading.

Beyond their love for each other, Sol and her husband have a genuine passion for adventure and exploration. Whether it's embarking on a thrilling hike through the mountains or immersing themselves in a new culture during their travels, they are always seeking new experiences that enrich their lives and deepen their bond.

That's when I knew all this was bullshit! Don't get me wrong, my husband has many interests. Like me, he doesn't sit still. But when the article said "He's adventurous and likes to explore," that's when I knew this smelled funny. If not for me planning family vacations, booking flights, and taking care of all vacation logistics to a destination country, my husband would be 100% content staying home all day long. He's not an adventurer and prefers to stay home surrounded by his daily comforts.

It's now 6 a.m.

I go upstairs where he's sleeping and woke him up and asked, "Drew, were you involved with this?" He was asleep and not really understanding what I was asking, so I explained to him what had happened. He got up, skimmed through the article, and his first response was, "Why did they leave out charming and good-looking?" We giggled, but then I got serious quickly. "Drew, I'm serious, did you have anything to do with this article?" He said, "No babe, I didn't, but send me the link; this is going to make for a great morning read."

I quickly went on LinkedIn and posted the link to the article and asked if anyone knew the CEO of the company. A dear friend of mine reached out and connected me to the CEO. We chatted via text and scheduled time to speak that afternoon. That was a good thing; the anger had subsided by then, and I was in a much better place to have a rational conversation.

Now usually my approach is to make margaritas out of lemons, but in this case, this was a personal invasion of my privacy. The article was about me and my husband, but neither of us were involved in writing it or approving it. (Truth be told, I was so thankful the article wasn't negative, defaming my career, my family, or his company. The situation could have been a lot worse.)

Afternoon came, and the CEO, his cofounder, my friend (who had brokered the introduction), and I hopped on the call. I explained my goal was not to sue or litigate but to genuinely understand what had happened.

The CEO was first and foremost apologetic. He took 100% accountability and immediately told me all the actions he had taken to remove the article from the Internet and de-index it from Google. That was a good start. Then proceeded to tell me:

- They are a company that's been around for a few years in the space of business intelligence (BI), they have a sizable development team, and they have a very small marketing team.
- The head of marketing was exploring new off-the-shelf AI tools to increase traffic to their website, increase impressions, and find ways to generate leads.
- They found an SEO AI company and followed their process. The tool would identify the top 100 keywords for their industry, create articles and blogs for each of the keywords, and post them across a variety of media channels to create market presence and traffic.
- The marketer agreed, and they began the trial.
- The AI company identified the top 100 keywords and generated six articles per keyword using their generative AI solution.

Sounds straightforward, right? Fairly harmless. Here's where things went wrong:

- When I asked how my name got involved, he said my name was one of the keywords that appeared in the "top 100" list under "business intelligence."
- I then asked who reviewed and approved the list before anything was done with it. He said "no one."

- With his head slumped and embarrassed, he told me the marketer did not review the keywords, nor did he review the articles associated with each of the keywords.

- Everything was autogenerated, there was no "human in the loop" to verify anything, and everything was all distributed on the Internet without a single human approval. Ouch!

What's worse is the marketer logged into his dashboard to see the results of the SEO AI tool, and his impressions had increased by 60% and traffic had increased by 90%. So from his perspective and his KPIs, the AI tool was working.

It wasn't until the CEO approached the marketer that both realized a lot of the keywords and articles generated were junk. They didn't iterate, and there was no human involvement. Luckily, they acted fast, stopped the SEO AI engine from producing more keywords and articles, and removed all blogs and articles posted on the Internet.

All this happened because there wasn't someone verifying if the keywords were relevant and if the articles made sense. It was simple, silly, and could have been 100% avoided if common sense was applied and if the company had enforced "human in the loop."

What did we learn from this ordeal?

- "Human in the loop" is mandatory. You always need someone to review the results of any AI outcome before it gets passed onto a client or employee.

- For a moment, imagine if every company had leveraged this tool without reviewing the work. The Internet would be flooded with bogus articles. To make matters worse, imagine if something like this happened during election season, about a president. How would we identify fact from fiction?

- If machines are training on the data and these bogus articles are a data source, we have the potential of further perpetuating biases and falsities.

Scary stuff, I know; but I promise, it's not all doom and gloom. AI is beautiful in many ways. Just like anything else, you must take the necessary precautions when deploying it.

In the next chapter, we will dive into the positive impacts and advancements of AI across a variety of industries and functions. The next chapter serves as a basis to educate, inspire, and show us the advancements in the space that we may not even think were possible.

How AI Will Impact Every Industry and Function

Artificial intelligence has quickly become a versatile technology that has impacted a variety of industries and functions. However, different types of companies, industries, and functions are all approaching and adopting AI in a variety of ways and with different degrees of urgency. Just like cars have varying speeds and features, company size and structure are also influencing the speed and adoption. In this chapter, we'll discuss the following:

- The five (5) types of companies and their approach toward AI: blue chips, large private companies, small businesses, startups and scale-ups, and small business owners

- Ten industries and three use cases within each industry, for a total of thirty (30) AI use cases across industries

- Ten functions and three use cases within each function, for a total of thirty (30) AI use cases across functions

The Tipping Point for AI

Over the course of the book, I've shared with you a variety of ways in which AI is impacting businesses and our daily lives. While some may still think smart phones, digital assistants, and ChatGPT are the extent of it, AI has quickly become a versatile technology impacting a variety of industries such as agriculture, healthcare, and education, along with functions like procurement and marketing. The explosion can be attributed to a convergence of these three (3) key factors:

1. **Groundbreaking Algorithms** The development of novel and more advanced algorithms, such as deep learning, has enabled AI systems to acquire knowledge and solve complex problems in ways that were previously unimaginable.

2. **Data Explosion** The abundance of data accessible to AI systems is greater than ever before because of the ubiquity of the Internet and the increased utilization of cutting-edge sensors and other data-capturing technologies.

3. **Enhanced Computing Power** The potency of computers has been rapidly escalating, thanks to advancements in chip technology and the advent of cloud computing. This new-age computing power has allowed us to process volumes of data never imagined before and use sophisticated AI algorithms on our laptops whereas previously you needed an entire room full of IBM mainframes.

These three factors have come together to create a tipping point for AI. AI is no longer science-fiction fantasy; it's simply a tool that is being used to solve real-world problems and is a catalyst for transforming industries, functions, and small and large businesses alike.

Also, what we see may feel new, but in fact, artificial intelligence has been in research for decades (I'll cover this in more detail in the section "The Development and Jargon of AI"). For now, just know that what you hear, read, and listen to, has literally been in research decades. For example, ChatGPT was in research for nearly eight years, with the support of nearly $2 billion in funding, before it became an overnight success in November 2022.

AI is spreading and reshaping our lives, just as email transformed communication, phones and apps created global communities, and Excel and Word became essential tools for personal and business tasks. From healthcare to manufacturing to education and retail, no industry will remain untouched with time. Even functions like legal, HR, supply chain, and customer service have felt its impact. It's only a matter of time before small businesses such as dentist offices, coffee shops, boutique stores, bakeries, and gyms adapt to this era of innovation as a means to outsell their competitors and scale their operations.

In this chapter, we will delve into the various industries and functions that have been touched by the transformative power of AI. The goal of this chapter is to expose you to what's already taken place and being explored, to help educate and inspire you, as well as to help you assess the following:

- What of this is relevant for my business?
- What is our risk tolerance, and how much can we take on?
- What pace is right for us?
- What can we realistically tackle considering our organizational maturity?

All of this feeds into your "why," your purpose, your strategy, your use cases. After all, you don't know what you don't know; this chapter will help you with that so you can think through how to best be prepared for your business, yourself, and your teams.

NOTE Becoming obsolete is only a matter of time, so find the rogue in you, be bold, think through the possibilities, and take charge of your path.

How AI Is Impacting Various Businesses

Everywhere you turn you hear AI this and AI that, but despite the omni-presence of AI in public discourse, its practical applications and impacts vary greatly across different industries and sectors. At times it may feel like every company is using AI and they are all doing ground-breaking work, but the reality of it is, some are, but most are still exploring, and it's a lot of marketing hype (for now).

Don't get me wrong, considerable progress has been made and there are remarkable offerings in the marketplace, but it's crucial to recognize that most of these developments and advancements primarily cater to a small segment of the market. The majority of companies are still cautiously testing the waters, experimenting, and implementing a handful of use cases as proof of concepts. Consequently, only a handful of real AI applications have transitioned to full-fledged production.

There's also a distinction to be made between the types of companies and their sense of urgency in approaching and adopting AI as part of their organization. This is probably applicable to you. Just as there are different types of cars with varying speeds and features, companies, industries, and functions also have varying speeds and approaches toward embracing AI. For simplicity's sake, I have classified them into five categories: blue-chip public companies, large well-off private companies, small businesses, start-ups and scale-ups, and small business owners.

Blue Chips

Blue chips are companies that are known for their stability and reliability in the market. They are generally highly risk averse and prioritize protecting their profit and loss (P&L) statements and reputation. These companies understand that their brand image is crucial to maintaining their position in the market, and any negative publicity or failed project can have a significant impact on their stock price and earnings per share (EPS). As a result, blue chips tend to be cautious and selective in their approach toward innovation. While blue chips recognize the need to evolve and adapt to changing market conditions, they do so with caution. Companies such as Walmart, Kroger, and Ford understand that experimenting with new technologies or business models can have a significant impact on their production lines, product delivery, or customer service operations and that any disruption to these critical business functions can result in lost revenue and decreased shareholder value.

Therefore, blue chips tend to be more conservative and prefer to wait until new technologies have been thoroughly tested and proven before implementing them into their business operations; while they experiment with a ride range of POCs, very few see the light of day in production until years of development have been in place. This is why I personally call developing innovations within blue chips *perpetual POC purgatory*. This "friend zone" is where, sadly, most innovations and experiments live. It's where most of my innovations and creations have lived, and it has taken a considerable amount of time for me to convince execs that the reward outweighs the risk. If I had to summarize the ratio of time I spend building versus convincing, I spend 70% on communicating and selling and 30% on building and deploying within enterprises.

Well-Off Private Companies

Private companies operate differently from publicly traded companies. They have more flexibility to experiment with new technologies and strategies without the pressure of meeting quarterly earnings or pleasing shareholders. However, this doesn't mean they are reckless in their approach to innovation. In fact, these companies are just as careful and deliberate in their decision-making process, especially when it comes to implementing emerging technologies like AI. Mars, Bechtel Corp, Chrysler, Cargill, and IKEA are just a few examples of well-off private companies that have the size, resources, and freedom to explore AI applications in their businesses. However, they do so with caution and careful consideration. These companies understand that AI has the potential to revolutionize the way they operate and compete in the market. They also know that it comes with risks and challenges, so they are cautious, deliberate, and can be as conservative as blue chips in their approach.

Small Business Operations

Small business operations are the backbone of any economy. They are the growing companies bringing in millions in revenue, supporting local employment, and always bringing in new ideas, products, and services to the market. They constantly innovate and pivot to stay ahead of the competition and bring in new talent and mindshare. By default, they also have a lot more flexibility in that they can make quick decisions and are willing to try new things to stay ahead of the curve. Their ability to embrace AI is a lot easier and faster, but their challenge is that they often lack the time or maturity to do so. They are busy taking care of existing clients or nurturing prospects and barely have enough capacity to develop new capabilities. Additionally, many growing small businesses do not have well-defined business processes. This can make it difficult for them to take advantage of the automation and augmentation capabilities of AI.

What I've observed over my years is that this is very much a chicken-and-egg situation, and it may as well be for you too. Small businesses need to invest time to get back time, but time is the one resource they often are insufficient in.

Start-Ups and Scale-Ups

Start-ups and scale-ups are a unique breed of business entities and stand apart from traditional corporations. Companies that fall into this category are usually characterized by their innovation, so they have different business objectives and different risk tolerances. This typically ushers in great talent who doesn't want to be confined to the processes, rigidity, and bureaucracy of larger companies. Also, their focus is different.

The goal of a start-up, for example, is getting a product out to market as fast as possible, and it doesn't have to be perfect. This prioritization enables the organization to launch products quickly to seek immediate consumer feedback, which is very different from the approach of private and blue-chip companies.

Moreover, start-ups and scale-ups are known for their cutting-edge technology and AI-fueled culture, so adopting anything new that helps them cut through the noise and distinguish themselves is a plus. As a result, they are well-equipped with the latest technological advancements, allowing them to stay ahead of the curve and remain competitive in a rapidly changing business landscape. This attracts investors as their unique offering can yield significant returns for the investors.

The challenge with start-ups and scale-ups, however, is that they may cease to exist in two years as they struggle with consumer acquisition, commercialization of their products, providing returns, and distinguishing themselves in a sometimes-saturated market.

Small Businesses

Small businesses are what we encounter in our daily routines and lives, be it our dentist's office, chiropractors, dry cleaning, java shops, kiddy-care, or education. Their core purpose is to provide services to fulfill our community needs, and employees often consist of the owners, family members, high schoolers, and citizens of the community. They are the mom-and-pop shops trying to make ends meet. At this moment in time, AI hasn't really penetrated this segment of business, and many believe it won't. However, AI will inevitably tiptoe its way in because AI will impose itself on all businesses. It's not a question of if, but when. How will you be prepared?

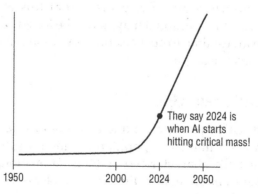

They say 2024 is when AI starts hitting critical mass!

1950   2000   2024   2050

How AI Is Impacting Industries

Now that we have a baseline knowledge of different companies and their speed of adoption, let's dig into how AI is impacting companies at an industry level. McKinsey estimates a total annual revenue impact of nearly $9 to $15 trillion across a variety of industries, of which I've outlined 10 of several in the following sections.

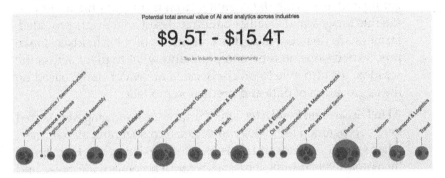

While my list is not comprehensive, I chose these 10 industries specifically because they are unassuming in nature. After all, we all know banks and financial institutions are leveraging AI (i.e. fraud detection), but how are industries like agriculture or food and beverage thinking about and experimenting with AI?

In the sections to come, I'll give a brief explanation of each industry and the ways in which AI is being used.

Your goal is to use this knowledge and think through ways in which AI can be applied in your business, while leveraging the six-phase AI deployment framework I provided in Chapter 4.

It's important to note that throughout this book I've purposely left out tools, vendor, and company names; I think it's important for me to stay vendor agnostic, and tool agnostic. For the purposes of illustration, however, I may mention names we're familiar with, but in no way am I sponsoring or promoting vendors and tools.

Agriculture

The agriculture industry grows crops and raises animals for food, materials, and/or other products. It involves a range of tasks from planting seeds to harvesting crops, as well as managing livestock. It's the primary source of the world's food supply, and every human depends on the grains, fruits, vegetables, and livestock that are produced. It's also the primary means for many countries and their economy. These days, however, agriculture is not just about traditional farming; it has expanded to include a variety of modern practices that improve efficiency and productivity due to the increasing population and food demands. Once an industry that was owned and controlled by famers only, agriculture has evolved to leveraging robotics, precision science, and AI-based livestock monitoring.

- ▪ **AI in Precision Farming**   This industry is leveraging AI by aggregating and analyzing data coming from farm equipment, drones, satellite images, and weather patterns. Based on the data provided, farmers are then assessing the conditions of their fields to make precise decisions on where to plant and what to plant across the seasons. It's also able to precisely calculate water usage based on the aggregation of data and prediction models.

- ▪ **AI in Disease and Pest Detection**   Farmers are leveraging AI-powered image recognition technology to detect, recognize, and alert farmers when specific diseases and pests are affecting their crops. Farmers are then proactively treating the issues before it becomes widespread and affects their crop yield and their revenue.

- ▪ **AI in Agriculture Robots**   Robots equipped with AI are performing a variety of tasks including weeding, fruit picking, and harvesting. They work alongside humans to increase productivity and counteract any issues with labor shortages, which occur often in this industry. Robots have increased their output and have been a great risk mitigation tactic.

Source: Fue et. al., 2020 / MDPI / CC BY 4.0

Travel and Leisure

The travel and leisure industry has evolved too. It's no longer about traveling for fun or relaxation but now includes a variety of products and services to provide an entire experience. The industry is hyper focused on personalization and consumer experience. Highlighted here are a few examples of where AI is being used in this industry:

- **Facial Recognition**   Airports and hotels are using facial recognition technology to streamline the security and check-in processes, reducing wait times and improving the customer experience. If you have Global Entry, Clear, or have used KLM as an airline, you'll notice they use facial scanners to identify passengers. This is all AI at play.

- **Chatbots and Virtual Agents**   Travel companies are using AI-powered chatbots for customer service in an attempt to provide 24/7 service. The chatbots are trained to answer certain tasks such as making a reservation, changing a reservation, and handling some (not all) customer requests without human intervention. In cases it cannot complete the function, it routes you to the right department. While I would say not all chatbots are created equal, and some are extremely frustrating to work with (I personally have a tendency of yelling "Customer Service" more often than I care to), the chatbots do help with basic tasks.

- **Dynamic Pricing and Route Availability**   Ever notice how airline prices are all miraculously in sync? Either flights and hotels are very expensive or travel seems to be affordable. This is because the travel industry relies heavily on AI algorithms to analyze market demand, competition, and external factors such as weather, events, conferences, and destination trends so they can adjust prices in real time for flights, hotels, and travel packages. This helps them maximize their revenue and competitiveness. This is where the advancements in this space does not benefit us directly, but thanks to several websites like Kayak and Google Flights, we also have the advantage to compare airlines and hotel prices, so touché!

Manufacturing

The manufacturing industry is booming and probably one of the most exciting spaces for me. The advancements I've seen from Industry 2.0 to now 4.0 is impressive, and I'm excited to see how this industry evolves as there is so much opportunity ahead. At its most basic level, manufacturing is about taking raw materials (metals, chemicals, and materials) and transforming them into finished products and goods that we use every day like mops, vacuums, TVs, hair products, makeup, office supplies, and more. The transformation from raw materials into finished goods goes through a variety of processes from fabrication to assembly lines.

Manufacturing, like agriculture, is under immense pressure to produce more goods but in a safe, cost-efficient, and eco-friendly manner. We're very much a buy-based society. For example, if we think about the use of robotics in assembly lines for car manufacturers, this has dramatically increased the speed, safety, and efficiency in production. The same principles and technological advancements are now being applied toward all consumer goods from fabrication (cutting, bending, and mixing raw materials) to machines (drilling, shaping, and painting) in order to meet the expectations of consumers at a scale that is humanly impossible. The following are some examples as to how AI is being applied in manufacturing:

- **Predictive Maintenance**   Manufacturing plants have a lot of equipment to manage and maintain, and keeping it all in production is key to how many products they can produce in a single day. As such, they have adopted robots, sensors, and AI to continuously analyze data coming from these sensors so they can predict when an equipment needs maintenance or when a solvent needs to be replaced.

- **Quality Control and Inspections**   AI systems have been deployed for precise visual inspections of consumer goods. The systems detect flaws, defects, and inconsistencies in products at a speed and precision that is unmatched by human ability.

- **Robotics**   AI-powered robots have been performing tasks for manufacturing companies at scale since the late 70s early 80s. The robots perform repetitive tasks, work with hazardous materials in hazardous environments, and can handle materials with precision, creating a more productive and safer work environment. Additionally, these robots collect data and can send information back to operations for better forecasting and formula perfections.

Retail

The retail sector is expansive and constantly shifting, facing a great deal of hardship in today's economy because of competition, cost of goods, and customer expectations with the omnichannel experience. Whether you're a boutique or a national chain, in modern times you're expected to provide optionality via physical stores, e-commerce, and over-the-phone service. With elevated customer expectations, retailers are being squeezed, so they've begun leveraging AI to meet the never-ending demands.

▪ **Personalized Recommendations**   Whether on Amazon or Zara, any interaction online is being analyzed to better understand your shopping patterns, click-throughs, and page views. The system is deterministically mapping your preferences to provide product recommendations that are relevant, increasing your cart size and purchase amount.

   Now, in the case of recommendation engines, they vary greatly. In my experience, I've had the pleasure of deploying three massive recommendations engines and studied many models before, and I've learned, no two models are alike. Also, I've learned some companies do it better than others. At the most basic level, companies can deploy a recommendations engine without using AI. They simply use a decision tree model such as "If customer chooses a red blouse, offer black slacks." However, great recommendations engines leverage AI and factor in multiple considerations such as past buys, current trends, seasonality factors, user preferences, and shopping price points. The difference between an OK and a great recommendations engine is using basic descriptive analytics (as in the case of the red blouse) versus machine learning (studying and learning about your many preferences).

▪ **Chatbots, Crawlers, and Bots**   Chatbots are providing customer service and resolving issues 24/7 without the need for human staff. Crawlers and bots are scouring the web and analyzing customer reviews, competition, and social sentiment. This information is guiding retailers to align their offerings with trends, giving birth to what we now call *fast retail*. Ever wonder how runway trends make it into everyday stores so quickly? This is how.

▪ **Virtual Try-Ons**   AI is powering virtual fitting rooms where customers can create a digital image of their body based on their measurements. Customers can then try on clothes without having to actually go into the store. The technology can assess the size, cut, and style against the customer's body shape, reducing the rate of returns, and lifts sales through AI automated recommendations based on the persons shape and size. This advent was accelerated during the COVID-19 pandemic.

Media and Entertainment

The media and entertainment industry encompasses a wide array of activities that involve the creation, production, and distribution of content across television, newspapers, streaming services, social media, virtual reality (VR) experiences, and more. It's rapidly evolving and arguably the industry that's being disrupted the most by AI due to the conflict between artists and machines.

With the invention of generative AI, nearly anyone can write a book, become a poet, write a screenplay, create a production video, produce a beat, and distribute content. What used to be in the hands of experts is now democratized to the masses with generative AI, causing massive disruptions that have led to Hollywood strikes, legal questioning of copyrights, and companies suing OpenAI for copyrighting infringement.

While I'm no subject-matter expert in media and entertainment, I did spend some time in the industry as the Executive Vice President and Chief Data Officer for Sony Music. What I witnessed in the music industry was that it's full of talented artists, managers, and creatives who conjure original works of art based on imagination and inspiration. But just as artists get inspiration from past works of art, machines get their generative abilities from past works of art but in different forms such as images, MP4 files, text, or audio. So, how we define what is original work versus what is not won't be easy moving forward, and I'm personally curious to see how this industry evolves. With that said, here are some use cases that the industry has thoughtfully deployed to remain competitive but not overstep the creative boundaries of artists:

- **Enhanced Gaming Experience**   In the gaming industry, AI technology is used to create more realistic, complex, and adaptive gaming environments. AI is influencing nonplayer characters (NPCs) to react in a more humanlike ways, making recommendations to players and creating worlds based on real-time player interactions.

- **Content Creation and Moderation**   There is a surge of user-generated content with the AI tools available to us all. Humans can create content at speeds and with graphic imaginations never seen before. However, the cost is we're blurring the lines between factual and nonfactual content, which is the reason we need monitoring. Fake news and personal points of view are flooding the Internet and training the AI models too. As such, we need to be careful and invest heavily into monitoring data to ensure we quickly identify and remove inappropriate or inaccurate information so we avoid training AI models on biased and harmful data. We've already seen cases where bias is injected into marketing content.

- **Targeted Advertising**   AI is being used to analyze consumer data, media channels, and content outlets to better understand user preferences and behaviors allowing media companies to serve their ads at the right time, in the right place, and to the right users.

    These are the "socially acceptable" use cases of AI in the media industry. The following are "socially debated" use cases. It's important to understand why AI is creating disruptions in this industry so you can also think through implications in your industry.

- **Deepfakes**   AI has the power to create highly realistic and convincing digital faces and voices. This has the potential of being very harmful in geopolitical arenas and during presidential campaigns because we as a society won't be able to tell fact from fiction.

- **AI for Music Composition**   AI algorithms have the power to analyze music patterns, beats per minute, top 100 songs on Billboard charts, and famous artists across genres to generate new music, melodies, and lyrics in seconds. All this culminates into AI-created music. In fact, a few years ago we thought two very famous artists, Drake and The Weekend, collaborated on a track only to find out it was AI-generated.

- **Influencers and Characters**   AI is able to crea virtual influencers and characters on social media. These characters are interacting with children, teens, and adults and have the ability to shape and influence how we think and what we buy and to create trends that can cross the line between physical reality and virtual reality, potentially harming our fragile society. This is something to think about for the future generations to come.

Healthcare

The healthcare system is a complex industry, presenting both obstacles and opportunities across the payer, provider, patient ecosystem. The industry encompasses a wide range of services from preventing, treating, and managing illnesses to mental and physical preservation and clinical support. Telemedicine and personalized medicine are even newer advancements. However, navigating this ecosystem is complex, highly regulated, and involves close collaboration among healthcare providers, insurance companies, government legislation, and patient advocacy groups.

Regardless of your individual beliefs on the efficacy of our healthcare system, the objective has always been to increase our life expectancy and enhance the quality of life for our family and friends. While some can argue that the basics haven't been mastered in this industry, healthcare is still taking a leap forward and exploring a variety of AI use case.

- **Robot-Assisted Surgery** AI-driven robots are assisting surgeons, increasing the precision and accuracy of the surgery, getting better results, reducing patient recovery times, and reducing post-surgery malpractice cases.

- **Wearables** AI wearable devices are being deployed in clinics, hospitals, and in-home services to accurately monitor patients' health post-surgery, responses to medications, and the progress of chronic illnesses. These devices can provide real-time data to healthcare providers and treatment facilities to provide optimal care.

- **Expediting Clinical Trials** Both digital and AI capabilities are being deployed to automate the clinical trials process, analyzing a massive volume of data to increase the speed of drug discovery, create new therapies, and reduce the cost and time to market.

Other more exploratory areas where AI is being deployed include the following:

- **Disease Diagnosis and Predictions** AI algorithms are analyzing medical imaging data, patient data, global economic conditions, and geo-famines to predict outbreaks, catch early signs of disease, and provide more accurate diagnosis of cancer, diabetes, and heart conditions.

- **Personalized Medicine** Although still new, personalized medicine and longevity trends are taking shape for the health conscious. Options are being provided to tailor treatment plans based on the individual's health data, family ancestry, and genetic makeup.

Consumer Electronics

This industry is exciting and catering to ordinary citizens, and we get to feel and see AI at play, every day, without even knowing it. We're essentially living in an era where it feels as though we've seamlessly adopted a futuristic lifestyle. We're living the Jetsons' life! From the launch of the Roomba in 2002 as the first robotic consumer product to innovations like Siri on our mobile devices, Alexa in our homes, Tesla's Autopilot in our vehicles, Nest Thermostat to control our homes, and Apple's Face ID for personal security, we are seeing AI at play everywhere. It has had profound changes in the way we communicate and the way we manage our homes, our tasks, and abilities to stay connected. Although the industry faces constant challenges with the pace of rapidly changing technology, we're no doubt the benefactors of the outputs. The following are listed use cases:

- **Smartphones and Apps**   AI is enhancing our user experiences with our smartphones by providing table-stakes features such as voice assistants, camera enhancers, personalized tracking, predictive text and voice recognition, and the countless apps we have available to us that help us with pick-ups and drop-offs, shopping, and reminders.

- **Smart Home Devices**   AI-powered devices like smart thermostats and smart security systems can be preprogrammed but also learn our behaviors with time and auto-adjust the settings to meet our needs. While many of the devices work remarkably, some still can't solve the age-old husband and wife problem of different temperature preferences.

- **Smart TVs, Voice Assistants, and Smart Speakers**   AI is embedded in a variety of our devices helping us customize our preferred settings with voice controls and commands, enhanced picture and sound quality, and audio recommendations through adaptive learning.

Fashion and Apparel

In the present, the fashion and apparel industry includes much more than just fabricating and supplying apparel and footwear to consumers. The industry involves supporting eco-friendly and green choices, keeping up with innovations on assembly lines, branding, marketing, coming up with dress styles and sneakers that simultaneously fit buyers' taste while providing optionality as trends take shape, inventing fast retail, and aligning with the vast array of consumer segments that exist in the world today. The pace of change in the fashion and apparel industry is one of the fastest, influenced by both cultural and social norms and environmental factors. AI use cases include the following:

- **Trend Predictions**   AI is used to analyze data coming from social media channels, runways, TikTok hashtags, and media portals to predict fashion trends for fashion and apparel companies, sending the prediction signals to design, assembly, and fabrication teams. On average, it takes two to four months to see trends from runway shows in fast retail stores like Zara, Forever21, and major department stores. This is remarkable considering all the logistics involved in turning a concept into a piece of article hanging at your local retailer.

- **AI-Powered Stylists**   AI tools are taking your measurements, creating virtual avatars, and asking a series of style preference questions to make recommendations for articles of clothing and footwear across a variety of e-commerce sites that match your budget, style, and figure. They even allow you to try on the clothes virtually through your avatar. You no longer need to be an actress, a musician, or a wealthy individual to have your own stylist; everything is available digitally and with a click.

- **Sustainable Fashion**   AI is being used to inspect garments during production to ensure quality and consistency of the fabrication but also to help brands track and manage their environmental footprint, promoting sustainable practices in the fashion industry, which is a space the younger generaton is deeply concerned with and interested in promoting.

Education

The education industry is burdened with slowness and complexity, yet it holds colossal power over the personal development, social thinking, knowledge acquisition, and critical thinking skills for the generations to come. The industry has evolved past traditional classroom settings, embracing remote and online platforms, digital technologies, and personalized learning approaches thanks to COVID-19.

Like healthcare, however, the industry faces many challenges. The norm has been a very "peanut-butter" spread approach toward education versus evolving to accommodate a variety of learning styles and disabilities. Another challenge is the growing skills gap between what is taught in schools and what is required in the job market.

The education industry, in addition to media and entertainment, are arguable the two industries being disrupted the most by AI. With the advent of generative AI and the accessibility of ChatGPT, teachers and institutions need to rethink their approach to learning. Old ways of memorizing and synthesizing are no longer an effective means to education with the advent of AI. While the industry is still contemplating the path forward, there have been some advances in the space that are embracing AI.

- **Education Chatbots and Learning Platforms**   AI-driven chatbots are assisting students with questions, helping them with mathematical problems, and offering help in the learning process. Learning platforms like Khan Academy are leveraging generative AI capabilities to interact with students at their level of vocabulary and education level. It asks the students questions and responds in ways in which the student can relate. It also actively analyzes the data on a student's performance to identify areas where the student is struggling and offers improved teaching methods.

- **Language Learning and Higher Education**   Because of the increasing number of online platforms, AI is being embedded to help curriculums by converting a variety of lessons into multiple international languages, offering personalized lessons, using voice recognition for pronunciation practice, providing interactive exercises, and tailoring learning materials to meet the pace at which students learn.

- **Personalized Learning**   Although still a bit new, I've seen AI being applied to tailor learning materials to meet individual disability needs and learning styles. It's able to auto-create content (including textbooks and online courses) and help track student outcomes to help parents and educators intervene with learning progress and at-risk students.

Food and Beverage

The food and beverage industries are largely focused on the production, processing, distribution, and sale of food and drinks. It's one of the first industries to adopt the automated assembly line, and the industry is heavily influenced by consumer preferences for healthier options, sustainability, and convenience. What I've seen disrupt this industry the most is due to population demands, changing tastes, generational preferences, and food science; the industry is constantly adapting and releasing products for mass consumption with a high risk of failure and cost implications. Remember Coke's release of New Coke when it was trying a new recipe? Or the Heinz's colored squirt ketchup available in blue, purple, and green colors because market research said kids like color? Both were financial disasters.

Furthermore, the industry has strict guidelines with food and safety controls, making it an industry that's very conservative with experimentation but always open to innovation when it comes to increasing productivity. Examples of AI applications in this industry include the following:

- **Quality Control and Inspection**   AI systems are being deployed to inspect and sort foods on production lines ensuring quality controls are in place to meet safety guidelines and that everything complies with health standards.

- **Food Safety Monitoring**   When food or beverages have been contaminated, the cost of bad PR and global recalls are massive. Therefore, AI is being used to proactively catch and detect food-borne illnesses, agricultural hazards, pesticide claims, and more, allowing companies to react in real time, pause production, and redirect assembly lines until the issues have been resolved.

- **Waste Reduction**   As our population grows and we continue to consume at exponential rates, our need to be precise with food and beverage production has heightened to avoid further waste. As such, AI systems are being deployed to optimize portion sizes, optimize and predict shelf life, and create exact ingredient measurements to optimize waste production.

Environment Health and Safety

The environment health and safety (EHS) industry is relatively new to the AI world but slowly picking up adoption. The industry focuses on ensuring safe and healthy working conditions, minimizing environmental impacts, ensuring workplace safety, ensuring public health, and implementing environmental protection laws at local, national, and international levels.

Although this industry is not as advanced as some of the industries mentioned earlier, it is starting to adopt AI into its operations to manage the micro-complexities of the industry. AI applications include the following:

- **Hazard Identification and Quality Monitoring**   AI algorithms are being deployed and leveraged to process a variety of data types coming from workplace cameras, air quality devices, and water collection units to measure and proactively monitor the presence of real-time hazards, pollutants, waste, and poison.

- **Emission Control**   AI is helping monitor greenhouse gas emissions across local and national territories where industrial processes are vast and industries like livestock, manufacturing, fashion, and retail are prevalent.

- **Wearables**   AI models are being deployed at hazardous work sites, requiring employees to wear wearables to track and measure drops in heart rates to detect sleepiness, elevated health indicators to indicate anxiety, and dehydration to avoid employees from passing out. The goal is to reduce the number of accidents, injuries, and law suits that commonly happen at work sites.

Conclusion

As you can see from these 10 industries, AI is influencing businesses in a variety of ways, at different paces, and each with its own unique advantages and disadvantages. Some are forced to evolve faster than they would like, as is the case with education and media and entertainment. Others are adopting AI at a pace aligned with consumer expectations, as is the case with consumer electronics.

Either way, all industries are exploring the change and looking to adopt AI. They may be in different stages of the process, and depending on their risk tolerance, size, and exposure to obsoleteness, their pace at examining, discussing, formulating strategies, and experimenting will be different. Learn from cautionary tales such as Nokia, Motorola, Blockbuster, Kodak, Xerox, and numerous other companies that failed to stay relevant. Action, whether it be slow or fast, is a must, and all industries are getting started.

How Artificial Intelligence Is Changing Functions

Like industries, functions are being impacted by AI. In departments like HR or procurement, AI is introducing new efficiencies in how employees manage their tasks and workflows, streamlining processes that are traditionally time-consuming and prone to human error due to bad data entry.

In this section, we will dive deeper into 10 business functions and my experience across the different departments. I will outline ways in which AI is reshaping these business practices, bringing about a shift (albeit slow) in how organizations have historically viewed these functions. Let's begin.

Legal

Whether you have a legal department or outsource your legal work, legal plays a crucial role in that it provides legal advice, helps with dispute resolution, advises on intellectual property rights, performs contract reviews, upholds employer employee agreements, and much more.

The legal industry is conservative and traditionally slow. By nature, most of the work is manual and performed by lawyers who have spent decades in practice and don't plan on changing. However, with the advent of ChatGPT and other generative AI capabilities, the industry has been shaken up a bit because they are forced to make sense of how to govern AI, create new copyright laws, and protect the rights of intellectual property (IP) used to train machine learning models.

So, by and large, while the legal industry is one of the slowest functions to adopt to any change, I am seeing AI adoptions across smaller practices with a younger workforce. Some examples include the following:

- **Contract Review and Analysis**   AI tools are being used to review contracts, highlight potential issues, and suggest modifications. While lawyers are still skeptical that AI tools know "the law" better than them, some are exploring these tools to summarize long contracts and get an executive summary, saving them hours in a day and allowing them to service more clients.

- **Legal Research**   Like Google, legal departments are using AI tools to help expedite the research process by using these tools to sift through vast legal databases to find relevant case laws and statutes needed for litigation. This speeds up the discovery process.

- **E-discovery**   AI tools and chatbots are sorting through electronic data (emails, PDFs, text logs, event logs, and more) to find relevant information related to a legal case.

Procurement

The procurement department is responsible for overseeing the acquisition of goods and services needed for business operations. This includes negotiating contracts, managing supplier relationships, and ensuring timely delivery of goods and services.

If you take a look at their day-to-day responsibilities, it includes identifying and selecting vendors and suppliers, discussing terms and conditions, creating and managing purchase orders, managing costs and stock levels, and continuously assessing suppliers to manage risks associated with supply chain disruptions.

Like legal, procurement is also slow to adopt AI, leaning heavily on the workforce and individuals to manage communications, collaboration, and connectivity of all the daily tasks. However, some companies and their procurement departments are leaning heavily into AI to build efficiency and speed as their demands for new vendor and supplier relationships increases, but their headcount allocations remain stagnant. The following are examples:

- **Contract Analysis**   Like legal, procurement is leveraging AI to perform first-glance rudimentary contract reviews, scanning for key terms and conditions and bringing to surface unfavorable contract terms. With the quantity of statements of work (SOWs), master service agreements (MSAs), and addendums they have to read, AI is helping the procurement department stay afloat and uncover details they often miss due to the heavy workload.

- **Vendor Risk Management**   For some procurement departments, working with the right vendors and partners is critical to maintain their company's public image. As such, procurement departments are using AI to set up alerts on pre-existing relationships to ensure any public announcements and news don't have an impact on their company's stance in the marketplace and don't disrupt their supply chain.

- **Compliance Monitoring**   Although this is not as popular, I've seen some procurement departments that operate in sensitive or highly regulated industries use AI to monitor and track updates and changes to compliance and procurement policies impacting their industry. This allows them to stay up-to-date with the changing demands and be proactive with planning and preparing.

Project Management Office

I don't know about you, but I've historically relied heavily on my project management office (PMO) for both small and large projects. When done well, business leaders, stakeholders, and project teams get a clear view of progress, timelines, milestones, forecasts, risks, assumptions, budget, workforce utilization, project burn rates, and delivery estimates.

While the project management (PM) space has been flooded with a variety of PM tools and there is no shortage of options, these tools are starting to embed AI to rethink how projects are managed and making the process more efficient, data-driven, and aligned with business objectives. The following are a few AI-based examples:

- **Risk Prediction and Management**   Current project management tools are embedding AI models that identify and predict potential risks based on the project data entered. The good ones even suggest mitigation strategies and pinpoint where the risk points are occurring. This type of insight can't be identified on Excel, Microsoft Project, or even with some of the current PM tools we use today.

- **Resource Allocation Models**   AI tools are also assisting with resource allocation models. By using data such as skillsets needed, resources assigned, resource rates, and resource bandwidth, AI model provides you with an ideal resource mix to make sure you hit your opex and capex targets and your timelines and that individuals don't get over-utilized putting project deliverables at risk.

- **Task Automation**   AI is also being embedded in a variety of PM tools to help automate repetitive and time-consuming PM tasks. These include sending emails to remind team leads to submit their updates, scheduling meetings, setting reminders for project deadlines and deliverables, syncing calendars, and generating reports.

Human Resources

The human resources (HR) department is a critical component of any business. My experience has been that they are often short-staffed, their needs get deprioritized, and they have the least tools available to them. However, this team manages some of the most critical operations such as recruiting and staffing, training and onboarding, employee relations, benefits and compensation, compliance, employee development, workforce planning, HR policy development, and exit management.

HR is seasoned with experienced HR professionals who are valuable to companies yet not the most tech-savvy. The function as a whole is not tech-centric, AI-centric, and data-centric when compared to their sister functions, but in my humble opinion it can benefit the most from AI to be more efficient. Why? I've worked with small and large HR teams, and most operate with Excel, sending along password-protected files in email and working off pivot tables. There's a lot of opportunity to advance this laggard space. The following are recent examples of AI being applied:

- **Resume Screening and Candidate Sourcing**   AI algorithms and models are looking through hundreds of resumes, selecting keywords, reviewing experience levels, and filtering candidates who have the most suitable qualifications for recruiting teams to review. While the HR teams are grateful for this efficiency, candidates need to be smart about how they write their resumes to ensure the needed keywords are embedded.

- **Chatbots for Employee Questions**   While this AI application isn't suitable for small businesses, it can be of great benefit for organizations that have several hundred employees where fielding employee Q&A can be time-consuming for the HR team. Chatbots are being created, trained, and made available to answer questions, provide links, and give specific information related to benefits such as holidays, paid-time-off policies, government forms, promotion cycles, and more. All of these are currently managed one-on-one via email, which is both time-consuming and burdensome for HR reps.

- **Predictive Recommendations**   This is probably the most exploratory space and use of AI among the three. It hasn't hit critical mass yet due to the limitations of data availability within HR. However, in cases where it has been deployed, AI models are being used to predict employee turnover and causes for leave, gather employee sentiment, predict workforce productivity to influence recruitment efforts, analyze skillset investments, and ensure that diversity and inclusion initiatives are being incorporated into the hiring practices.

Customer Service

Of all the functions mentioned in this section, customer service is the department that is experimenting with AI use cases by volume. Nearly all, if not all, industries are discussing or deploying AI across their customer service teams due to the growing number of daily calls, 24/7 service expectations, and intricacies of questions being asked by the younger generation.

For example, at one of my companies, callers were constantly asking questions like these: Which products are vegan? Which products have hyaluronic acid as a plumbing agent? What are the active ingredients of product X? When will more of this product be available? Whether you're a seasoned customer service rep or new to the floor, it is impossible to remember the details of every product across 80,000 SKUs and keep up with new product launches or the decommissioning of products. This is a perfect space to leverage AI and create a virtual assistant.

Furthermore, I learned it takes a minimum of six months of training before a new hire can take calls on their own. As such, companies are looking to expedite the process by creating knowledge stores that allow reps to field customer calls with accurate details.

For these reasons, AI applications have become popular within customer service and have been in production since 2011. They happen to be some of the earliest deployments of Watson. The following are some examples:

- **Knowledge Base**   Companies are aggregating product data, service data, customer complaint data, and data from databases, Excel spreadsheets, websites, and PDFs to train virtual assistants. This way, when customers call with specific or obscure questions, customer service reps have a knowledge store available to them that allows them to type in a question and get an answer. I've learned over the years that with companies that started this journey earlier, they are now making these knowledge stores available to the public through their website in order to reduce the number of incoming calls. However, they've spent years training the models, with humans in the loop, and confidence in the accuracy of the data presented. It's advised that companies just starting the journey deploy it as an internal knowledge store first to avoid any unintended consequences.

- **Sentiment Analysis**   Based on my experience, the second most popular AI use case is sentiment analysis. Companies are using a variety of AI tools to convert calls into text and running a sentiment model to determine the topic, satisfaction, and sentiment of the call. They are "tagging" and "categorizing" the calls to get quantitative insights as to the reason people are calling versus relying on their reps to tell them what they feel. This is a great way for companies to get an understanding if call volumes are due to product concerns or a specific marketing campaign, and they proactively address it through communications.

- **Triaging**   AI is being applied across both 1-800 numbers and Contact Us pages to categorize and route customers querie to appropriate departments, anticipate customer issues based on prior call or web activity, and enable customer support across a variety of languages.

Sales

By far this is one of my favorite functions with clear business benefits with AI. Not only is the value easy to prove, but the time efficiencies are also obvious, and the risk exposure is minimal so companies small and large are leaning into this function.

Sales is responsible for generating revenue; it's a driving force behind business growth. From lead generation to customer outreach, contract negotiations, market analysis, and product demos, the sales function is at the tip of the arrow for all businesses small and large.

Because it's the first line of defense, the function has always struggled with time management, balancing sales targets with building deeper client relationships and adapting to changing consumer needs. Not to mention, sales reps, like HR reps, aren't known for being the most tech savvy; a lot of the work they do is manual in nature and therefore time-consuming. That's why the applications of AI in this function have been so impactful and the time efficiency gains are obvious and provide business value. See the following examples:

- **Customer Calls and Follow-Ups**   We've all experienced countless sales calls and the time-consuming process of the follow-up email. We organize our notes, recap decisions, outline next steps, assign tasks, and set reminders for ourselves to follow up with prospects, clients, and teammates. I've measured this process on several occasions (for benchmarking purposes) and determined it takes a sales rep anywhere from 28 to 46 minutes to complete the follow-up email (excluding distractions from multitasking). If a sales rep has 4 to 6 sales calls a day, that's nearly 2 to 4 per day, 10 to 20 hours per week spent on this one activity. With the adoption of recent AI tools, however, calls are being recorded (like Zoom or teams), audio is being converted to text logs, and AI models are analyzing the logs to summarize meeting notes, outline key decisions, write up next steps, and draft the email for you. With great tools, I've even seen the tool match the voice with a name and assign tasks to specific individuals. I use this capability in all my calls, and it gives me back approximately 20–30 hours a week.

- **Sales Presentations**   Sales reps create countless presentations for prospects and clients, another very time-intensive activity. However, with recent AI tools, the tools can create a presentation template, insert web research on the company and industry research, and customize the design to match the client's website logo and color themes. This capability alone is saving teams anywhere from

6–13 hours a week. The thing to remember here is that there must always be a "human in the loop." The tool should not replace your role in crafting a succinct narrative, but it should help you automate and jumpstart the presentation process.

▪ **Personalized Sales Messages**   Another popular AI use case is content creation that can be sent through email and other communication channels to your prospects and clients. This is major horsepower for your reps because they can get through more work in less time. Instead of creating messages from scratch and treating each email as a one-off, the AI tools are creating the content, templatizing the content by type, and sending emails on your behalf as a follow-up. The only warning here is that you must, no exceptions, review the emails before they are sent. Remember, AI isn't perfect, and humans definitely aren't, so check the work to make sure the content is appropriate and relevant before clicking Send.

Training and Development

Like HR, the training and development (T&D) function within companies is often short-changed when it comes to getting adequate budget to help develop capabilities, identify skills gaps, fulfill training needs, and create and develop materials for career growth. However, much progress has been made over the past seven years because of the new data privacy laws and ethics courses companies are mandating, giving birth to a new space called *edtech*. It's where education and technology integrate and online learning platforms are making education globally accessible across a variety of languages. So, while traditional training and development functions within large companies have yet to adopt at the speed of the edtech space, what it is doing is leveraging these learning platforms as a means to catch up and ensure their employees are trained and informed. The following are a few examples:

▪ **Intelligent Training Systems**   AI models are being embedded into e-learning platforms to track learning styles and pace. There's usually an up-front assessment (just a few minutes) to assess how best a person learns; then it curates the content, speed, and exams accordingly.

▪ **Content Generation and Curation**   AI tools are being deployed to ingest, aggregate, train, and learn about company data. From that, the tools are creating curated content for different departments and their workforce. This allows the sales team to be informed of the latest product releases, newest specs, and competitive market research. It allows finance to be aware of the cost of goods and the financial makeup of markets, channels, and distribution centers. It allows employees to be aware of the latest product launches and corporate strategy. What I've seen over the years is that this is a great way to train the workforce at scale; however, the necessary evil is documentation. Everything needs to be documented for the AI tools to learn, and this is often where companies fall short. You're only as good as the data that's been documented.

▪ **Interactive Skill Development**   With the competitive landscape being as fierce as it is, companies need to ensure their workforce stays relevant with the latest skillsets. As such, AI tools are being deployed to help predict future skillset requirements, assessments are being done to identify current skills, and plans are being developed to bridge the gap between the workforce composition today versus where it needs to be over the next one to three years to stay competitive and relevant. From here, the e-learning platforms create personalized curriculums to adjust to the skills gap and learn through the interactions for more effective retention and engagement.

Finance

The finance function is one of the most complicated functions I've ever had to encounter over the course of my 25-year career. Outside of the sheer number of Excel spreadsheets they use to manage their forecasts, the number of departments within departments is astounding. I've never been able to get a single answer from a single source. I'm constantly being referred to subdepartments. Regardless of my experience, this function is pivotal to any organization, big and small, as it oversees a variety of financial activities, including budgeting, opex versus capex allocations, forecasts, cash flow, expense management, payroll processing, tax filings, and financial reporting to your board, the SEC, and investors. The reality of it is, over the course of my 25 years, I've observed that most finance teams run on Excel despite having all the algorithmic and modeling tools available to us as of 2024. It's crazy but true! To add flame to the fire, this function is also very conservative. Disrupting the status quo is not welcomed, and it's rare they change their processes. As such, the function overall has been slow to adopt the latest advancements, but I am seeing some critical mass in the following areas:

- **Expense Categorization**   AI models are being deployed to review expenses, ensure line items have been categorized correctly, make sure they don't exceed the allowed spend threshold, and flag anomalies, speeding up the expense process. It's not the sexiest use case, but it's very functional for this department.

- **Financial Planning and Analysis**   I've worked closely with my financial planning and analysis (FP&A) teams across many of my organizations, and I admire their tenacity to stay in the field. I, for one, could not do what they. In my years of exposure, I learned that FP&A is a key function for many brands, labels, and business units as they run all the financial reports and provide the forecasts. They use things such as price point, historical sales volume, cost of goods sold, operational expenses, exchange rates, inflation rates, and seasonality factors to develop their forecasts. But in today's economic conditions and with the pace of change and competitive threats, the volume and complexity of drivers have expanded. As such, the teams have to take into consideration competition (new and incumbent), social sentiment, generational preferences, labor costs, regulatory changes, local/market laws, import taxes, interest rates, consumer spend, and more. AI is being used to help them identify all these new factors.

- **Budget Allocations and Forecasting**   It's no surprise companies big and small have several strategic initiatives running in parallel, competing for the same bucket of funds. Finance is looking to AI to help support which spend will generate the most business value. AI algorithms are being deployed to analyze historical financial data, business outcomes, value generated, and revenue growth versus productivity gains to help create a variety of simulations and determine potential outcomes and to help in the decision-making process of where funds should be deployed.

Research and Development

Although I haven't had too much interaction with research and development (R&D) over the course of my career, my last two positions as CDAO and CAO brought me closer to this function. I got to collaborate and create with the department, and I have immense respect for what they do. I learned that this function is really at the core of driving innovation within an organization. Whether its creating new products or services, improving existing ones, testing new materials and methods, or pure discovery, this team is really at the forefront of a company's ability to stay relevant and competitive. What's ironic is we often view the tech space as being at the forefront of innovation, but I would argue that R&D is. My mind was blown at what they've been able to accomplish: discovering new drugs, creating environmental-friendly products without sacrificing quality, and developing new solvents that are heat resistant withstanding rising temperatures. The discoveries take years of experimentation and patience. For those reason, this department has my respect, and best, they are not shy about experimentation. The following are some examples of how AI is being deployed within R&D:

- **Material Science** The use of AI in chemical synthesis represents a major leap forward in the field of chemistry, leading to advancements in material science, like IBM's RXN for Chemistry. AI models are essentially trained in organic chemistry and chemical compositions, and then through machine learning, and the models are helping discover new compounds to improve synthesis processing, reduce waste, and discover new environmentally friendly compounds. Many industries such as pharmaceuticals, consumer products, and retail are leveraging this capability in product development.

- **Molecular Modeling** AI deep learning algorithms can predict how different molecular structures associated with drugs, food, or chemicals in our environment will interact with biological targets in our bodies. In essence, AI in molecular modeling simulates a three-dimension structure of a molecule and screens the molecule against billions of compounds; this process that usually takes years now takes months. The simulation then predicts the likelihood of impact and efficacy, helping researchers focus on the most promising candidates to test in real biological tests. Such was the case with Atomwise, a technology that helped companies screen billions of compounds to find those that could bind to and inhibit the main protease of SARS-CoV-2, the virus that causes COVID-19.

- **Optimizing Reaction Conditions** AI algorithms are being used to test how different variables such as temperature, pressure, and solvents are affecting the outcome of a chemical reaction. The models assess billions of variations, identifying patterns and correlations that would otherwise take human chemists' decades to explore manually. This helps accelerate the optimal set of conditions to maximize yield, increase efficacy, reduce negative reactions, and predict outcomes in various conditions. This data is then used by chemists and researchers to target where to start with their lab work, shrinking discovery times from decades to years.

Marketing

Like sales, marketing is another function where AI is being leveraged in day-to-day activities, and it's moving fast, almost too fast. Mistakes are being made daily, and I'm personally involved with helping marketing teams put in place processes and governance to ensure mishaps are reduced. Part of the issue is that a lot of AI tools removed the barrier to entry for marketers, making it too easy to do the work, so marketers are rushing into things without putting in place proper governance protocols. This is similar to what I shared in Chapter 6.

While there are dozens of AI applications in marketing, for the purposes of this section, I'm keeping it simple and limiting it to three safe applications, helping marketing teams accelerate their work with increased effectiveness. See the following examples:

- **Programmatic Advertising** In programmatic advertising, you buy and sell ad inventory in real time through a bidding system across a variety of ad platforms such as Google, Facebook, and Trade Desks. Based on your audience and preferred advertising channel, the system gives you the price per impression, and when you accept, you get to place your ad. As you can imagine, if not done right, this can be quite costly with minimal return on investments. You spend money on ads but without any real sales conversions. As such, AI tools are helping marketers analyze target audiences and channels to identify consumer segments that will drive lower cost of acquisition with a higher impression rate.

- **SEO and Website Optimization** By leveraging machine learning and natural language processing, many AI tools in the marketplace can help you improve your online presence and rankings in search engine results. It seems like a no-brainer, but you'd be surprised how many companies aren't leveraging these capabilities. AI tools are helping with relevant keywords for ads so you can outperform your competitors and suggesting content to lead to better search engine results.

- **Automated Email Marketing** AI tools are helping marketers write emails at scale that do a better job with customer acquisition by personalizing subject lines, writing the body of text, embedding images, and performing A/B testing to see which emails drive conversion. Marketers still review anything that goes out (remember the "human in the loop"), but the AI tools are operating as assistants accelerating their work.

Conclusion

As we close out this chapter on the diverse applications and roles of AI across various industries and functions, I hope that the insights shared have not only enriched your understanding but also sparked a flame of curiosity and ambition. I wanted you to see how different companies, industries, and functions all have taken up different approaches and adoption rates when it comes to AI. In the case of AI, one size does not fit all!

Your exploration of AI isn't just about grasping its current state but about envisioning its boundaryless possibilities. As you can see from the examples I have shared, AI is not a distant concept but a tangible tool that is enhancing every aspect of our lives, whether we know it or not. As such, expand your awareness, foster critical thinking, and embrace your options with an open mind, and you will find yourself not just following but leading in the age of AI. This is your moment to find the rogue executive in you and think bigger, dream wider, and step confidently toward a horizon brimming with possibilities.

AI Jargon and Development

From the beginning, we've learned that whether you're a leader or practitioner, you must find the rogue in you and be bold, make decisions, and present a case in a thoughtful, methodical, and logical way to evangelize and begin deploying AI in your organization. You've learned how to develop a strategy, ideate and select use cases, and prepare, solution, and deploy AI in a safe way that involves a "human in the loop."

In this chapter, however, we're going to get you grounded on the fundamentals of AI. It's more academic in nature, in that it's intended to teach you jargon, terms, and definitions. Along with what AI really is and is not, and a lesson in history, how we ended up here and the decades of research that went into.

What Is AI?

The world changed in November 2022 when OpenAI released ChatGPT. ChatGPT was the first commercial AI product available to the masses, including college students, business executives, and individuals alike.

It was accessible to us mere mortals and for free when all prior AI products were for businesses only (i.e. B2B).

When AI is done right, 1 + 1 does not equal 2; 1 + 1 equals 3 because of its tremendous amplification effect. Poet Ralph Higson once said, "Some things have to be seen to be believed," and this is 100% true when it comes to AI.

Like many things, when you're describing a song, a picture, or a beautiful landscape, to grasp the beauty and essence of what's being explained, you must be there witnessing it, hearing it, or seeing it with your own eyes. The same goes with AI. It's so powerful that you must see it in action to fully understand it.

For example, what if I told you in 1996 that you would have access to a cool communication tool that allows you to send messages to anyone, anywhere, anytime and you never have to pick up a phone again? Here's how it works:

1. You can access this tool from your computer at anytime from anywhere.

2. You click Compose or New and write your message in the designated area. You can add attachments like digital pictures or documents to the file.

3. You can send this message to anyone, but you must have their "email address," which acts as a unique identifier for that person.

4. Once sent, your device sends the message to a central server via the Internet.

5. The server receives the message and delivers it to the recipient's email server.

6. The recipient's email server then delivers the message to their email address on their device, where they can read it in their inbox.

Describing email as a capability doesn't have the same impact as actually seeing it in action. Could you really grasp its power as I described it? No. The same goes for AI.

That's why AI is transformative and shaping our future in unimaginable ways. It has the power to amplify human capabilities and create outcomes that surpass traditional expectations, and with the growing demands of our world, it's the only way to keep pace. So how did we get here?

What Is *Not* AI?

Before we can begin, it's essential for everyone to have a basic under-standing of what AI is and is not. This may sound boring and your eyes may be glazing over right now, *but* it's needed because people make stuff up all the time. They pretend to know something because they read an article in the *New York Times*. Let's not be that person! At a minimum, know what you're talking about so you're not a poser, and come from a place of knowledge and understanding.

To start, I will walk you through some terms, definitions, and con-cepts in "plain English" and with a lens that's approachable and easy to understand. It won't matter if you're a dentist, a teacher, or a business owner; you'll understand the concepts and terms and start deciphering what's what in the world of AI. Let's begin.

To begin understanding AI, you need to have a basic understanding of computer science. Computer science, like history or liberal arts, is a subject. But instead of learning about the Civil War or philosophy, you learn about computation: how computers work, how information is processed by computers, and how algorithms can be created by com-puters to solve everyday problems. Artificial intelligence at its core is a branch of computer science. It's focused on programming computers to create intelligent machines capable of solving problems and performing tasks that would typically require human intelligence. For example, AI can do the following:

- Recognize patterns in large amounts of data that would take humans days, weeks, or months

- Learn from experience and make informed decisions using data it's fed and being taught right from wrong

- Adapt over time, continuously improving and allowing the com-puters to accomplish tasks with minimal human intervention without needing sleep, food, or time to see a loved one

All of these functions are created and trained by humans at the onset until the models have been trained well enough that they can perform the tasks and make decisions on their own. It's similar to teaching a sec-ond grader addition. At first, it's difficult, but with homework, practice, and adult supervision to help you, the student learns. Eventually 3 + 3 becomes 6 and it's automatic, without thought or time.

This is how training the computers is working today, so understanding the fundamentals of computer science enables you to better appreciate how AI works, how it's shaping the world, and how to get prepared.

The Difference Between Artificial Intelligence and Human Intelligence

Artificial Intelligence (AI) and Human Intelligence (HI) are different in their origins, processes, capabilities, and limitations. Human Intelligence (HI) has evolved over thousands of years. It's inherently biological, mostly developed to survive and thrive threats, and it results from neural networks in our brain.

AI is a man-made form of intelligence created and programmed by humans. It's based on algorithms and computational processes through computers.

HI is developed by learning through experiences, observations, and social interactions. Our genetics play a major role in our inherent characteristics, and our ability to problem-solve is through abstract and lateral thinking. While human learning is highly adaptive and flexible overall, it has limitations due to our emotional needs, well-being, and physical needs (like sleep).

AI learns from data. Therefore, the person providing the data and teaching the machine acts as a caretaker, like parents and children. AI can generate novel solutions to specific problems, but within the specific parameters of the data it's fed. The power lies in the fact that computers have nearly no limits on how much data they can take in, absorb, and memorize; but computers *are* what you feed them. Computers can therefore quickly develop biases and preferences if the data they are fed is biased or unclean.

Furthermore, HI has the ability to process ambiguous and incomplete information, because we've developed intuition, have abstract thinking, and can understand context, tone, and emotional queues. We have social intelligence that allows us to navigate through complex social and political relationships.

AI, however, runs on a different fuel: data. So, while it excels at processing large volumes of data quickly, it requires explicit instructions to effectively operate. The output is only as good as the input, so the input needs to be accurate enough. This is why "prompt engineering" has become a common phenomenon.

In summary, while AI can mimic certain aspects of human intelligence and it can exceed human capabilities in specific tasks with greater accuracy and speed, it lacks inherent biological, emotional, and ethical complexities that characterize human intelligence. It only learns from the data we provide, so we have the responsibility of ensuring what we feed it has social value, which has led to the field of responsible AI, which we covered in Chapter 6.

So, while there are differences between HI and AI and inherent strengths and limitations with each, artificial intelligence has advanced so much in the past 10 years that as a society we are now fearing the gap between the two forms of intelligence.

Jargon, Terms, and Definitions

Terms and definitions are being thrown at us in every direction. Whether your source of information is from LinkedIn, Gartner reports, McKinsey studies, news feeds, academic publications, or basic passerby information, it is nearly impossible to keep pace with everything. Terms like *machine learning, neural networks, ChatGPT,* and *natural language processing* are becoming increasingly ubiquitous. As these terms gain prominence in our daily lives, it's crucial for us to cultivate a basic understanding of what they mean and how they are being used to shape this space.

In the following sections I've outlined a few terms and their meanings. This by no means is exhaustive, but it will cover 80% of what you need to know. I've provided both the technical definition (but in "plain English") supported by an everyday example so you can translate the meaning into everyday application.

Computer Science

Computer science is an academic field. Similar to art history, mathematics, or business administration, it's a field that focuses on the study of computers to understand programming languages, algorithms, and architecture, and how to convert these principles into both software and hardware solutions. You can see its application in everyday life when you're browsing the Internet, looking at social media, and using any app that's on your phone. Without this field, the Internet, Uber, DoorDash, Netflix, and Google wouldn't exist.

Computer Scientist

Computer scientists are individuals who have either studied computer science or have chosen this as their profession. Not all computer scientists are equal, though. There are many verticals within computer science including software development (like websites), research and development (developing new computer languages), machine learning (discovering and/or using different algorithms to analyze large sets of data), architecture (making sure software and hardware integrate, like your phone with your downloaded apps), and more.

You can see its application in everyday life when you're using a search engine like Google, new feeds on Instagram without searching for it, Amazon providing you with recommendations on products, your ability to buy a phone and sync it with your iCloud, and cloud systems like Google Drive and Dropbox syncing from anywhere in the world. These common conveniences were all created by computer scientists.

Programming

Programming is what computer scientists "do" to develop software, hardware, applications, and systems. Programming is the process of creating instructions to tell a computer how to perform a task, which involves writing code in a variety of languages such as Python, SQL, Java, and C++. Just as humans speak different languages, programming comes in different languages to help the computer create the algorithms, software, hardware, video games, graphics, and apps for your phone.

Code

Code refers to a set of instructions written in a programming language that tells a computer what to do. Each language (i.e. Python, SQL, Java, C++, and so on) has its own rules, structure, and meaning that dictates how code is written and interpreted. For example, if I wanted to write a line of code that told a computer to "take Consumer Name in column A and combine it Loyalty Number in column B," you'd see something like these examples, shown in two different languages:

SQL Language

```
SELECT A. ConsumerName II "," II B.LoyaltyNumber AS NewValue FROM
Consumers
```

- A.ConsumerName refers to the consumer name from Column A.
- B.LoyaltyNumber refers to the loyalty number from Column B.
- The II operator is used to concatenate the two values (Name and LoyaltyNumber).

- AS NewValue gives a name to the new value you've asked it to create.
- FROM Consumers specifies where the data is being taken from.
- In this example, the capital letters are the instructions telling the computer what to do, for example, SELECT that, JOIN this, etc.

Python Language

```
ConsumerName = ['Alice', 'Bob', 'Charlie'] # Example data from
Column A
LoyaltyNumber = ['123', '456', '789'] # Example data from Column B
CombinedValue = list(zip(consumername, loyaltynumber))
```

- ConsumerName is a list containing consumer names in column A.
- LoyaltyNumber is a list containing loyalty numbers in column B for the consumers in column A.
- CombinedValues is instructing the code to create a new list by combining the two earlier lists.

As you can see, both sets of code are instructing the computer to do the same things but in different languages and ways.

Algorithm

An *algorithm* is a series of steps or a set of rules designed to perform a specific task or solve a specific problem. Writing code and using an algorithm are closely related, but they refer to different aspects of the process of programming. Algorithms are more about the logic or strategy behind solving a problem and are language agnostic, meaning it doesn't matter what programming language you use. Premade algorithms have personally been a game-changer for me and my teams. Off-the-shelf models and algorithms speed up results because we don't have to write all code from scratch. The focus is on efficiency and helping coders and noncoders alike perform a set of functions.

In everyday applications, an algorithm is like a recipe, a bit of information prepackaged and ready for use by anyone without the need to know a programming language, while code is the step-by-step act of implementing the recipe in a specific language (i.e. English, Spanish, French, etc.).

Data

Structured Data

Structured data is data that has a standardized format that can be efficiently read by both humans and computers. Think of your Excel sheet: there are tabs, rows, and columns. That is structured data in a nutshell. Computers can effectively and efficiently process structured data at massive volumes and speed to extract insights because of its quantitative nature.

Unstructured Data

Unstructured data is data that does not have a predefined structure nor is it organized in a predefined manner. It cannot be stored in a traditional row-column database or an Excel spreadsheet. It comes in the form of images, videos, and audio files (i.e. music).

Semi-structured Data

Semi-structured data is not structured or unstructured data; it's a combo since it has a structure but doesn't conform to rigid structure like a database or Excel spreadsheet. Types of semi-structured data include emails, zipped files, and web pages.

Data Engineering

Data engineering is a field that focuses on data discovery, collection, storage, and retrieval. It's the data engineer's job to build and maintain environments that allow analytics, data science, and computer science to ingest the data they need to train the models and seek the desired insights and capabilities.

Analytics and Data Science

Analytics

Analytics is a discipline that involves people analyzing data. It is used to discover, interpret, and communicate meaningful patterns in data to help you make meaningful decisions. Some also refer to this field as *Business Intelligence*. The goal is to take data and create patterns that you can then transform into insights for problem-solving and decision-making. The field of analytics can range from descriptive analytics to sophisticated techniques that support predictive and prescriptive analytics.

Examples of everyday descriptive analytics include fitness apps that track your steps, calories, and activity. Predictive analytics include traffic and navigation apps that tell you the time to the destination. Prescriptive analytics is being used to create movies and content based on watching and listening habits to influence.

The following is a summary of each type of analytics to help you understand the terms even more.

Descriptive Analytics

Descriptive analytics describes what has occurred already. It takes data from events or sales that have already occurred and gives you a view of what's taken place. As an example, a fitness app can tell you your average steps/week, based on the historical data of your average steps/day for the last seven days. Descriptive models help summarize a dataset and interpret the current state of affairs. These models are useful for gaining insights from historical data and often the primary model used for analytics in identifying patterns, trends, and relationships with data.

Predictive Analytics

Predictive analytics is a powerful branch of analytics that uses historical data, statistical models, and some machine learning algorithms to forecast future outcomes and trends. It's an approach to forecasting future outcomes, leveraging both historical and present data. It belongs in the "advanced analytics" realm. Think of it as peering into a crystal ball, not to see your destiny but to gain insights into what might happen based on patterns in the past. It relies on analyzing large sets of data and creating mathematical representations of the variables, parameters, and relationships within the data.

Prescriptive Analytics

Prescriptive analytics forecasts future trends, provides recommendations, and suggests actions to take to achieve a desired objective. It goes beyond predictions because it suggests a course of action. With prescriptive models, the maintenance is nonstop because you always need to feed it new, or what we call "live" data, to ensure the course of action aligns with the most recent course of events.

In summarizing the differences among descriptive, predictive, and prescriptive analytics, *Descriptive* answers the question of "What happened?" It provides you patterns so you can decide what happened in a current situation. *Predictive* analytics moves one step ahead in that it answers the question "What could happen?" by analyzing historical and transactional data to identify risks and opportunities to forecast or outline future patterns. *Prescriptive* analytics goes even one step further and answers the question "What should we do?" because it can suggest actions and provide recommendations.

Data Science

Data science combines math, statistics, programming, advanced analytics, and data engineering to uncover actionable insights from structured, unstructured, and semi-structured data. It's different than analytics, although they're related. It's a field that's evolved and is critical to our way of operating today and enables all the capabilities mentioned earlier. Harvard Business Review dubbed the data scientist the sexiest job of the 21st century.

In today's world, computer scientist and data scientists are developing nearly most, if not all, business capabilities involving AI. From using social media to run your digital campaigns to extracting sales pipeline insights from your CRM to measuring your health metrics on your iPhone, you have two fields of science that focus on analyzing data and building computer systems that facilitate, accelerate, and amplify everything we do in business.

AI Terms

Machine Learning

Machine learning (ML) is a subset of AI that allows machines to learn from data, and past experiences. It's a technique that uses algorithms to analyze and interpret patterns in data to enable learning, reasoning, and decision-making.

To simplify, basic analytics and statistics can answer questions like these:

- How much does my average customer spend?
- What day of the week do I earn the most?
- What week of the year is the most profitable?

However, when you're dealing with interactions that have a variety of variables such as seasonality, inflation rates, store hours, and level of advertising (print and digital), when using Excel or a statistical software, these variables won't have a relationship to the program or the naked eye. When using ML, however, you can discover hidden relationships so you can make sense of your operations and what is having the most impact on your gross sales.

Another example of ML is training it for image recognition. The machine takes images and deciphers the pixels. It creates a statistical pattern within the data to determine the difference between a cat from a giraffe. Machine learning is very powerful, but it also has limitations. A famous image I use to depict the inherent weaknesses of ML is its inability to distinguish the difference between a Chihuahua's face and a blueberry muffin. Funny, right?

Deep Learning

Deep learning (DL) is a subfield of machine learning that focuses on models that were created to simulate the neural networks of our brain, enabling the computer to perform tasks such as image and speech recognition and to communicate with us via natural language.

These neural networks are *deep*, meaning the models have multiple layers of analysis between inputs and outputs. Deep neural networks are known best for their ability to work with unstructured data (audio, image, sound, and free-form text), they require massive volumes of data to learn, and unlike the other models, they can make predictions based on new and unseen data.

In today's world, a perfect use case for deep learning is diagnosing disease from medical imaging like X-rays and MRIs. Something that is otherwise timely, costly, and labor intensive using standard human means is now globally scalable and more accurate, helping us in the preventative care movement.

Neural Networks

Neural networks (NNs) are a subset of machine learning and at the heart of deep learning algorithms. The name was inspired by the human brain where biological neural signals are sent to each other. Neural networks do the same; they consist of interconnected units (like neurons) that process data and pass their responses to the next layer of connected units.

Imagine it's Christmas and you have to decorate the house with tiny interconnected light bulbs. Each light bulb lights up in response to the signal it receives from the prior light bulb. If one light bulb is down, all light bulbs are down. NNs operate in the same way. In the case of NNs, however, a light bulb gets a signal to light up, but it also is told how bright and what color; it gets trained from the prior light bulb.

GPT

The *GPT* in ChatGPT stands for Generative Pre-Trained Transformer. This means the model that powers ChatGPT will "generate" coherent and understandable text based on your input. The model has also been pretrained on large datasets, so it understands language and context, and training is not required from the users' end. Lastly, "transformer" identifies the type of neural network that was used by the model. Together, it describes the conversational model that uses GPT architecture capable of generating human-like test responses and chats.

Natural Language Processing

Natural language processing (NLP) in its simplest form teaches computers how to understand, interpret, and respond to human language; it's the technique used in teaching computers how to read, listen, and even speak to humans in their own languages.

So, when you talk to Siri or Alexa and it responds, or when you type a question into a search engine and get an answer, that's NLP at work. It's all about bridging the gap between human communication and computer understanding.

Facial Recognition

Facial recognition (FR) is teaching computers how to identify and verify people by analyzing their faces. Just like you notice the color of someone's eyes or the shape of their nose, facial recognition allows computers to identify people based on various details of the person's face. The computer scans the face, noting unique features (like the distance between the eyes or the curve of the cheekbones), and then compares this "face map" to a database of known faces. If it finds a match, it surfaces the recognized person.

Prompt Engineering

Prompt engineering is the art and science of giving the right "instructions" to the computer model so that it can respond correctly without knowing code or any of the programming languages outlined earlier. It gives us "normal" humans the ability to communicate with computers to work effectively.

Just like a movie director's instructions have great influence as to how a movie is made, we as prompt engineers have great influence on how the computer understands what we're asking, and how to respond. The way you phrase a prompt can give you the difference between a short and scientific response and a long and creative response.

As examples, the following are two prompts using Gemini (Google's version of ChatGPT). As you can see, the differences in prompts make a difference in the output.

> **Prompt #1:** Briefly describe to me the meaning of Christmas. I want it factual and brief.

Christmas commemorates the Christian belief in the birth of Jesus Christ, which is traditionally celebrated on December 25th, rooted in ancient Roman celebrations and early Christian traditions. It evolved to encompass cultural elements like gift-giving, feasting, and decorations.

Key aspects:

- *It's a time for Christians to reflect on faith, attend church services, and celebrate the arrival of Jesus as a divine figure.*
- *Christmas combines religious significance with secular festivities, offering a time for reflection, joy, and cultural celebration.*

> **Prompt #2:** Briefly describe the meaning of Christmas and why it creates such joyous and happy times for families and friends.

For Christians, the birth of Jesus signifies hope, new beginnings, and God's love for humanity. This inspires joy, gratitude, and a sense of peace. Christmas traditions encourage connection, with church services, caroling, and gatherings bringing people together to celebrate their shared faith.

Key Aspects:

- *The act of choosing and exchanging gifts embodies generosity, spreading joy and strengthening bonds between loved ones.*

- *Celebrations and gatherings bring about festive meals, music, decorations, and traditions creating a shared joyous experience, fostering family cohesion and memories.*

- *Goodwill and charity often spark a spirit of giving back, promoting kindness and compassion towards others.*

Overall, Christmas offers a unique blend of faith, merrymaking, and connection, creating a powerful emotional resonance that fuels happy times for families and friends.

This is why Prompt Engineering has become such an important facet of AI with GenerativeAI. How you write your question and request, has a direct impact on the response you'll receive.

How We Got Here

Now that you you're familiar with the field of analytics, data science, and computer science, and you know AI jargon, terms, and definitions, let's give you a little history lesson on how AI was developed and how we got here.

The real application of AI dates back to the early 1900s with early myths and folklore depicting machines with human-like intelligence. If you've ever seen sci-fi films from all the way back such as *Metropolis* (1927), *The Day the Earth Stood Still* or *The Invisible Boy* (the 1950s), *Star Wars* and *Star Trek* films (the 1980s), or *I, Robot* (this century), you know what I mean. These are all movies of a world where humans and machines co-exist in healthy and not so healthy ways.

In all scenarios, however, machines possess an intelligence that allow them to run autonomously, with the intelligence often created by the hands of man. This is AI in short form. It's a machine that learns and adapts based on information it's provided. Similar to an infant who can't talk, walk, or reason at birth, but with time, it learns and adapts. AI is just that. It's a blank canvas with some prewired composites that absorbs and processes data; and as we continue to supply it with data and images and teach it right from wrong (i.e. reinforced learning), the machines begin to improve and develop to a point where AI can make informed decisions, showcasing moral reasoning and demonstrating intellectual capacities beyond human capacities because, unlike humans, machines don't need rest or food to stay alert, learn, and develop.

The truth is that machines don't need to sleep. Machines have infinite memory. Machines don't have neurological complexities and genetic dispositions that drive personalities, disorders, metabolic issues, and psychological scars developed from childhood. It's very monolithic in that way.

Like your upbringing, where parents, nature, and nurture all have an impact and influence how you develop as a human being, the same goes for machines. We, in this very moment, are acting as the caretakers of machines, instilling knowledge, values, and principles so that they can serve us effectively and positively. But, and there is a *but*, not all humans are good. Some are embedded with rage, jealously, evil, and greed—we know this by the current geopolitical climate that has thrown many countries into war.

This is where artificial intelligence can get tricky. Because unlike government leaders who have terms that expire or are assassinated or overthrown by the populous, machines don't experience turnover. There's no retirement, and their knowledge will be ever-expanding and increasing, along with its biases, preferences, and misinformation as we feed it, like humans. Therefore, as the caretakers and the programmers, we need to be very responsible and accountable for our actions, and that is why the topic of responsible AI is so important.

Going back to how we got here, in the next section we'll focus on the evolution of AI in the 20th century so you're familiar with some key moments and timelines in history.

Early 20th Century: Conceptual Foundations

The foundations of AI as a reality was really born in the realms of philosophy, mathematics, and early computing. Pioneers like Karel Čapek, Alan Turing, Arthur Samuel, and many others started planting the seeds with their work, creating a pathway for the art of the possible.

1921: The word *robot* was first coined by the Czech playwright Karel Čapek who released a science-fiction play called "Rossums Universal Robots." *Robot* in Czech means "worker," and the play depicts millions of manufactured worker men who were without souls and feelings that were "good for nothing, high-powered labor." The work introduced the concept of intelligent machines and artificial people being used as part of a workforce.

1929: The first robot was then built by Japanese professor Makoto Nishimura. He referred to it as an *artificial human*, and the robot was called Gakutensoku. Although the robot was rudimentary in form, Professor Makoto was a biologist who wanted to dispel Karel Čapek's depiction of robots as slaves to humans. He wanted to show that robots can be friends who can help inspire and help us celebrate humanity.

1949: Arguably the first AI book written was *Giant Brains or Machines that Think*, by a computer scientist named Edmund Callis Berkeley. Berkeley refers to robots as "mechanical brains" that can handle large amounts of data with great skill and speed, and the power is very similar to that of a brain. The "mechanical brain" can do the "work of hundreds of humans for the wages of a dozen."

1950: The Turing test was created by Alan Turing. It was a test created to determine whether a machine could exhibit intelligent behavior equivalent to, or indistinguishable from, a human. A judge would ask a question through text-based communication, not knowing if it was asking a human or machine. The judge would then have to distinguish the response as man or machine. The focus was to test conversational ability, reasoning, and natural language.

1952: Another breakthrough moment happened when a computer scientist named Arthur Samuel wrote the first checkers-playing program for the IBM 701 in 1952. The project was officially completed in 1955 and aired on TV in 1956. He taught the machine to play checkers, a game of strategy and what appeared to be nearly infinite possibilities. Man against machine was aired publicly. Going back to the theme of IBM not getting enough credit for what it's done for the AI space, Watson was also publicized in 2011.

1955: The phrase *artificial intelligence* was coined at a gathering at Dartmouth. An assistant professor in mathematics, John McCarthy hosted a gathering to clarify and develop ideas about thinking machines. He chose *artificial intelligence* as the name to depict the field. This started the period that began early development in AI programs like the Logic Theorist and ELIZA, exploring problem-solving and natural language processing.

Mid to Late 20th Century: Expansion, Growth, and Challenges

In the middle of last century, AI quickly became the topic of sci-fi movies, making it a bit more mainstream and the topic of many conversations. Programmers from around the world also jumped into the realm of AI. Robots were being built, autonomous vehicles were developed and tested, and AI got the attention of the U.S. government. Unfortunately, the initial optimism around AI led to inflated expectations. (Sound familiar? Ahem, 2023 and 2024.) This eventually led to disappointment and reduced funding, and some call this lull the "AI winter" because the downward trend post hype was so extreme.

However, I disagree. I think the critics try to make this moment marketable by excluding facts. What we know is that robots, algorithms, and cognitive computing were all being developed during this time. However, to make the capabilities work at scale, we needed the essentials: compute power and data. Neither of these was available in a cost-efficient manner. It was simply cost prohibitive, and chip technology had not advanced at the rate of AI capabilities. Similar to Google Glasses (also a flop), AI was simply too early for its times.

With that said, there were lots of advances in those decades; some notable ones include the following:

1958: John McCarthy (the Dartmouth math professor mentioned earlier) created LISP (aka List Processing), the first programming language for AI research, still in use today.

1959: The term *machine learning* was coined by Arthur Samuel (the computer scientist who created the first chess game).

1961: The first robot was put into use at General Motors in New Jersey. The robot, named Unimate, was the first industrial robot ever built, using a hydraulic arm that could perform repetitive and dangerous tasks deemed too dangerous for humans. It could safely perform tasks such as transporting die castings and welding parts on a car.

1966: The term *chatbot* first came into existence with the creation of ELIZA, a mock psychotherapist created by Joseph Weizenbaum. It was originally termed the *chatterbot*, a machine that used NLP to converse with humans but was later shortened to *chatbot*.

1966: The principles of deep learning as we know it today came into practice when the Soviet mathematician Alexey Ivakhnenko published "Group Method of Data Handling" in the journal *Avtomatika*.

1979: The first autonomous bot was brought to market. Its inventor, James L Adams, created the Standford Cart in 1961, but it wasn't until 1979 that the Stanford Cart successfully navigated a room full of chairs without human interference.

Late 20th Century: Rapid Growth

In the late 20th century, all technology prospered. The 1980s was a period of massive growth. Chips, robots, mainframes, models, and more were developing rapidly, coining this as a period of "AI boom." Investments and funding were abundant, focused research began in the space, and the use of self-learning machines, which were computers that were learning from their mistakes and making decisions, became a topic of interest.

The 1980s were focused on the revival, resurgence, and resurrection of AI, driving new algorithms to be created and increased computational power, and there were notable successes with a variety of use cases where computers were performing human tasks with better accuracy. So, the outlook of the market had changed.

The 1990s of course was more about the Internet boom, but this unexpectedly helped the AI movement. The rise of the Internet increased data availability, fueling AI advancements.

Then in the 2000s things really shifted; it was about the emergence of machine learning and AI integration. It was a shift from knowledge-based systems to machine learning–based systems, where systems were learning on their own from data we provided, and AI systems started seeing their way into a variety of industries such as finance, manufacturing, and healthcare.

In these decades, some great advancements took place.

1980: The first commercial product, XCON, came onto the market and was first used in New Hampshire. It was a machine with 2,500 rules designed to assist in the ordering process of computer systems that automatically picked components based on customer needs and requests such as memory, cabinets, disks, tapes, printers, CPUs, etc. By 1986 it had processed 80,000 orders with 95–98% accuracy.

1985: A drawing program known as AARON was showcased. Its inventor and artist Harold Cohen developed a computer program that drew original artistic images. It started with abstract drawings in the 1970s but then progressed into representation figures, murals, and more.

NOTE   Today's hype of generative AI was triggered when OpenAI released ChatGPT to the masses and applications such as Dall-E and Midjourney were released in the hands of everyone that could create original artwork and images. The world woke up to the possibilities of AI, and now everyone could dabble in original art. There were positive and negative reactions to this. The positive viewpoint was "Wow, a machine can really do this!" There were of course negative reactions from the creative community at large because it felt the software diminished their artistic creations. The irony is the capability of generating images via a machine was first created in the 1980s, not in 2023.

1986: The first driverless car was created and demonstrated in Munich, Germany, by Ernst Dickman and his research team. It could drive up to 55 mph on roads that didn't have obstacles or human drivers. They got a call by Daimler, and by 1994, their team released Mercedes 500 SELs that had the ability to change lanes and react to other cars in France traffic with a fully autonomous computer system control board, steering wheel, brakes, and gas pedal.

1987: Alacritous Inc. launched Alacrity, the first managerial strategy system that had 3,000 rules embedded to help make business decisions.

1988: A computer programmer named Rollo Carpenter invented Jabberwocky, the first chatbot that would have live conversations with humans.

1997: IBM's Deep Blue beat a human (the world's best chess player Gary Gasparov) in a live chess game that was aired on TV, becoming the first computer program to be better at a human in strategy and decision-making.

2000: A professor by the name of Cynthia Breazeal developed a robot called Kismet that was able to mimic human expressions and showcase "feelings" through the use of eyes, eyebrows, ears, and a mouth.

2002: The first household robot, Roomba, was released to the public. It is an autonomous vacuum with sensors that have the ability to vacuum your home without your guidance and is one of the most popular consumer products in existence.

2003: NASA landed two rovers on Mars, Spirit and Opportunity, that were able to navigate the surface of the planet without human intervention.

2006: AI was used in advertising and media buys to develop a better user experience through recommendations-based algorithms created by Twitter, Facebook, and Netflix.

2010s–Present: Modern AI

With all the advancements and research that have taken place in the past few decades, the pace of change has become exponential. We saw breakthroughs in deep learning and advancements in image recognition, speech recognition, and natural language processing. We're seeing progression from virtual assistants to recommendations engines with AI systems now becoming part of our everyday lives.

Now as time passes and the machines become more "intelligent," the ethical and social implications are of concern, as well as the long-term employment impact, society impacts, and disruptions to industries. While the future is bright with more inventions, conveniences, and capabilities to reach more consumers, the next few decades will also unfold a new set of social complications.

There have been a lot of advancements in the past decade, too many to name them all, so here is a curated list that reached some level of public mania:

2011: IBM developed Watson. Similar to Deep Blue, Watson beat two of the world's best *Jeopardy* players, Ken Jennings and Brad Rutter, live on air.

2011: Apple released Siri, the world's first commercialized virtual assistant, and made it available on every iPhone.

2012: Two researchers at Google, Jeff Dean and Andrew Ng, trained the first neural network, creating the ability to distinguish and recognize cats using unlabeled images.

2016: Hanson Robotics created Sophia, the first "robot citizen," with realistic appearances, emotions, and communication abilities.

2018: A Chinese tech group, Alibaba, created a language-processing system that was able to beat human intellect in a Stanford reading and comprehension test.

2021: The Silicon Valley–based company called OpenAI developed and released DALL-E, advancing AI's understanding of the visual world by creating images through human-based prompts.

2021: Meta launched Gato, an AI system that learns and performs many human-like tasks such as writing essays and playing games. This was the first showcase of "general-purpose" AI or, as some call it, "applied AI."

2022: Google released PaLM. This AI system can generate what seems like limitless creative text, trained on 540 billion parameters (ChatGPT 3.5 was trained on 175 billion parameters).

2022: FDA approved the first AI-powered medical device for breast cancer detection. While AI was being used in healthcare in a variety of ways, most were experimental or exploratory.

2022: OpenAI launched ChatGPT, its conversational AI model to the public. It caught the attention of nearly everyone with its generative

AI capabilities to be used as a virtual assistant, as well as do creative writing, image creation, conversational abilities, chatbots, and more.

2023: Google released GEMINI, an AI system that is designed to comprehend and generate content across a variety of formats such as text, audio, images, and video, offering a more comprehensive range of understanding. GEMINI is a successor to LaMDA and PaLM2.

Conclusion

While I've left out a lot of other inventors and research that's contributed to the evolution of AI in our society, this timeline gives you the gist of major events, happenings, and the people involved. At a minimum, you'll be the smartest person at the dinner table or at least know your facts about how we got here.

> **NOTE** While we can't predict the future, the fact remains that businesses, small and large, will be impacted. It's not a matter of *if*, but *when*.

We will see more robots and self-driving cars, we will further need to sharpen our critical thinking skills to set us apart, and industries as we know them, like education, will look fundamentally different in 10 years.

No matter where you stand in the spectrum of thoughts and opinions, AI will have a place in our world, so let's embrace the opportunities it gives us and make sure it's used for social and business good for generations to come. After all, we're the creators of artificial intelligence and the official caretakers of the path it takes within our society.

What the Future Holds

As we look ahead, it will be fascinating to see how this space will transform various aspects of our lives, including how we receive healthcare, what we're taught in school, how we interface with home appliances, and more. While I can't predict the future, I can make certain assumptions based on existing trends across industries and functions and with what big conferences like Davos and the World Economic Forum are presenting. At this point in time, it's safe to identify these as the emerging trends in the next five years:

Continued Advancements in Machine Learning Machine learning, the driving force behind most AI applications, is expected to continue its rapid development. We will likely see more sophisticated algorithms that can learn with less data, more accuracy, and greater efficiency. This advancement will make AI applications more accessible and practical for a broader range of businesses, and it will penetrate our daily lives without us even knowing it.

Expansion of AI in Automation Automation, already a significant application of AI, will expand into more complex and nuanced tasks. Beyond routine and repetitive tasks, it will perform higher-level cognitive tasks, which could revolutionize industries by enhancing productivity and creating new opportunities for innovation.

AI in Decision-Making   AI's role in decision-making processes will expand. AI systems will become more capable of analyzing vast datasets to provide insights and recommendations, aiding human decision-makers at speeds we've never seen before.

Management Consulting and Consultants   The value of an outside expert was always their expertise and experience. As knowledge becomes accessible and available to everyone, it could diminish the value of consultants and their market insights and market research. Will the gravity of their statistics be worth the sticker price moving forward? The industry of management consulting will have to evolve their value proposition and staffing model as workflows become automated (creating less dependency on consultants and offshore resources) and as market research and statistics become readily available.

Personalization at Scale   One of the most significant impacts of AI will be its ability to offer personalization at an unprecedented scale. From marketing to product development, businesses will use AI to understand and cater to individual customer preferences, leading to more effective and customer-centric strategies.

Advancements in Natural Language Processing   NLP is set to become more sophisticated, enabling machines to understand and interpret human language with greater nuance, dialects, and context. This advancement will enhance applications such as customer service chatbots and applications for the speech impaired, and it will integrate global communications by making conversations and text more effective and human-like.

Integration of AI with Other Technologies   AI will increasingly be integrated with other emerging technologies, such as the Internet of Things (IoT), blockchain, and 5G. This convergence will lead to the creation of smarter, more interconnected, and efficient systems, opening new possibilities in how businesses operate and interact with customers.

Ethical AI and Governance   As AI becomes more pervasive, there will be a greater focus on ethical AI and governance as there was with GDPR a few years back when data privacy was a hot topic. This focus will involve developing standards and frameworks to ensure AI is used responsibly, particularly in areas such as privacy, security, and fairness.

Growing Importance of AI Literacy   As AI permeates more aspects of business and society, AI literacy will become a critical skill. Understanding the basics of AI, its capabilities, and its limitations will be essential for business leaders and employees across all levels and departments.

Predictive and Preventive Healthcare   In healthcare, AI is expected to move beyond diagnosis and into predictive and preventive applications. AI will analyze data from various sources to predict health issues before they occur, enabling preventive care and personalized medicine, making "biohacking" benefits available to all versus just the rich and famous.

AI in Sustainable Development   AI will play a crucial role in addressing global challenges such as climate change and sustainability by analyzing environmental data, waste production, and resource use. AI will contribute to more sustainable business practices and help develop solutions to environmental issues.

The Rise of AI Ethics Officers   As ethical considerations become more central to AI deployment, the role of AI ethics officers or similar positions may become standard in organizations. These professionals will oversee the ethical aspects of AI usage, ensuring compliance with regulations and societal norms.

Broader Impacts on Employment   While AI's impact on employment has been a concern, the future may see a shift toward AI creating new job categories. As AI automates routine tasks, the emphasis will shift to roles that require human creativity, empathy, and strategic thinking, reshaping the workforce landscape.

AI-Driven Security Systems   In the realm of cybersecurity, AI-driven security systems will become more sophisticated in detecting and responding to threats and anomalies. These systems will proactively identify vulnerabilities and respond to security incidents in real time, providing a more robust defense against cyber threats.

Scalability   As AI applications become adopted and POCs transition into production, scalability will become the critical challenge that will be tackled in the next few years. Businesses will need to find efficient ways to scale AI solutions while managing costs and maintaining performance.

AI's role in creative industries, such as music, art, media, and writing, will continue to grow. AI will assist in the creative process, leading to new forms of art and entertainment that blend human creativity with AI's capabilities. A perfect example of this is the Coke commercial that was created by its marketing team using AI. It's one of my favorite examples of perfect harmony between man and machine. `www.youtube.com/watch?v=nSmNy9iLhZ4`.

Insurance and Liability Laws   As driverless cars, genetic engineering, copywriting tools, cognitive appliances, telemedicine, and drones become more pervasive, new insurance and liability laws will need to be written, and our approach toward litigation, mitigation, and settlements will need to evolve to accommodate the new tools.

Psychology and Mental Health   While most of the AI applications are still in research labs, we will see a surge of products hitting the market to help with virtual reality (VR) therapy, digital therapists, teletherapy, medication management, and cognitive behavioral therapy.

Small Business Owner Adoption   While most of the AI applications of today seem to be focused within high-tech, large public companies, large private companies, and small/midsize portfolio companies, we'll see a growing trend with small business owners adopting AI to help them with time-consuming tasks such as accounting, payroll, consumer data collection, mobile and website development, social media campaigns, payment processing, digital sales agents, media buying, and more. While small business owners are laggards now, within a few years the chasm of adoption will be crossed, and we will see critical mass with this segment of the population.

What Keeps Me Up at Night

While there is promise and hope and I'm excited to see what the future holds for us, I often get asked the question, "What keeps you up at night?" Well, there are a few things I'm maniacally observing.

Speed

I'm keeping my eye on the pace at which the advancements are occurring. Moore's law is in full effect, and the pace of change is exponential. I've been in this space for decades, and I've never seen this speed.

In fact, I can barely keep up. In the realm of technology, never have I seen such rapid and transformative growth as AI. Its evolution, its impacts, and the implications for businesses and humanity across the globe is astounding. AI has progressed from theoretical research into real-life applications that we use on our phones, computer, home appliances, and more. How? It's because of the advancements in these three specific areas

Computational Power   Computation power allows us to process large amounts of data, complex algorithms, and model at record speeds.

Data   The surge and influx of data being generated by our interactions with everyday appliances is astounding, all of which is being used to train these machines.

Machine Learning   Breakthrough tech like machine learning is allowing us to create machines that can detect images, converse with us in a variety of languages, and perform predictive analytics.

As a result, we can automate tasks, enhance, and speed up decision-making and personalize the customer experience in ways we've never been able to do before. While the capabilities are remarkable and I'm very optimistic about the value it provides, I do get concerned with the pace of change and our ability to keep up, making it an ever-changing, uncontrollable, and overly fluid environment.

The rapid development of AI presents both challenges and opportunities.

Cybersecurity   As reliance on AI grows, so does the risk of AI-powered cyber threats. We have to invest in robust cybersecurity measures.

Ethical Considerations   The rapid deployment of AI raises ethical concerns such as privacy and bias. Businesses must navigate these ethical considerations carefully. The challenge is that there is no black-or-white answer, so it requires careful navigation because of our diverse ways of thinking within society.

Skills Gap   As the AI revolution commences, we're in need of new skill sets, while upskilling the existing workforce. I wonder if with time, will we further bifurcate the skills gap between the haves and have-nots, or can we bridge the gap in an effective way?

Advances

I'm concerned about the progression from artificial intelligence to artificial general intelligence to artificial super intelligence. There's talk among us in this field about how long it will take to get to artificial super intelligence (ASI) now that AI has been democratized to the masses. Why is this important? The fears people have of robots taking over the world or humans being manipulated by machines is the work of ASI, not AI. Here is some background:

AI stands for **artificial intelligence**, machines programmed to perform tasks that typically require human intelligence. It can solve some problems, recognize patterns among a sea of data, and understand our language to the degree it was trained. As remarkable as it is, it predominantly is still narrow in its applications.

AGI stands for **artificial general intelligence**. It represents the future where machines possess the ability to understand, learn, and make decisions on their own across a wide range of tasks at a level comparable to humans. While AGI today remains theoretical, it is the next milestone in the AI evolution.

ASI stands for **artificial super intelligence**. It represents an AI system that surpasses AGI and doesn't require human intervention for results, answers, or outputs. It can improve upon its own intelligence and make decisions on its own. There's talk in our field that we'll hit ASI level capabilities by 2040 versus the original estimated 2050. That's less than 20 years away. Not to mention, we must tackle the monopolization of the technology and ensure its not the same five tech companies at the head of the helm.

As you can see, we are the ones shaping the future, creating the capabilities, and advancing the machines. We are the guardians of this ability, and it is our duty, like a parent with a child, to nurture it in the best way possible and ensure that we raise ethical, well-behaved machines with positive intentions in all possible endeavors.

While the future is full of promise and we should approach it with optimism, we must also be mindful of the rapid pace of AI development and take the necessary precautions along the way. We should take advantage of the opportunities presented to us while striving for governance and accountability for what the future may hold. The navigation is key in this point in history.

What's Next

As you can see, AI is not just a fleeting trend but a fundamental shift in how businesses operate and compete. The first and most crucial recognition is that AI is here to stay. It's becoming an integral part of the business landscape, driving innovation and efficiency across all industries, functions, and businesses small and large. Ignoring AI is not an option for businesses that want to remain competitive, which means embracing its potential and being prepared to adapt your business models accordingly. AI is no longer a distant future technology; it's here and a necessity for staying competitive and having line of sight for what's around the corner.

As such, I suggest the following:

■ **Find the rogue executive in yourself** and dare to do what most are scared to do and take the first leap. It won't be pretty at first, but nothing worthwhile ever is. You'll come out with some scraped knees and some bruised elbows, and you'll second guess yourself many times. But remember, AI is not just a technological tool; it's a transformative force that requires a strategic and innovative mindset and a commitment to continuous adaptation.

■ **Act now.** Whether you are just beginning your AI journey or looking to deepen your engagement, the time to act is now. Be the rogue and take the leap, evangelize, and transform your organization to harness the full potential of what it has to offer. As we discussed in prior chapters, outlining your strategy, overcoming talent challenges, and cultivating an AI-ready culture are the primary factors in determining your success and preparation for the future. Go through the following readiness checklist and find your path.

■ **Use this essential checklist** to carefully craft your plan of attack to ensure your success in a deliberate and thoughtful way:

■ Leverage the use cases I shared with you and the examples I've given throughout this book to think through the possibilities. Reflect and get a clear understanding of what AI can and cannot do for your industry or function.

■ Decide to overcome inertia and start your AI journey.

■ Take a minute and decide if you're ready to "go rogue." Whether as a leader or a practitioner trying to create change, you'll be faced with obstacles every corner you turn. Are you willing to defy the odds and dare to be different?

- Discover your "why." Make sure you have a clear understanding of why you're doing this.

- Take the "Readiness Assessment" to gain a better understanding of your current capabilities so you can be realistic about the type of AI you can deploy with success, via an AI strategy.

- Find your AI strategy and streamline and focus the ideation process of your use cases.

- Ideate and select your use cases. Choose the use case that is highly critical but least complex to deploy to increase your chances of success.

- Build the right team or know how to work with an inherited team. Look for the needed virtues (grit, ambition, and resilience) and work with the 10 AI archetypes in the right way.

- Don't skimp on the preparation in the design or solution process. Make sure you answer the questions in the essentials list, regardless of the depth and extent of discussions and decisions.

- Upskill your team. It's helpful to take some time and invest in training to upskill your team. It doesn't need to be exhaustive. Use resources like LinkedIn Learning, Coursera, or the countless free YouTube videos available.

- Create your change management plan. Implementing AI may require some or significant changes in your business, so deploy effective change management strategies, and don't shortchange the process.

- Always make sure there is a "human in the loop" to avoid any unintended consequences.

- Continuously monitor the performance of your AI application to ensure it's still meeting your desired objectives. Remember, you may have to iterate a few times at the onset and throughout to make sure it continually meets your business needs. It's never one and done.

- Be prepared to adapt your AI strategy in response to technological advancements or changes in business priorities.

- Address ethical concerns. Look for and be proactive in addressing ethical concerns that might not be obvious.

- Join industry consortia or forums to stay abreast of the latest trends and best practices in AI. There are hundreds of AI newsletters you can sign up for to keep you up-to-date with the latest and greatest. A simple web search will give you a list.

- Form academic partnerships. If you really want to take it to another level, collaborate with universities or research institutions for access to the latest research and talent in AI.

I hope this book lived up to its name and will become your AI survival guide as you navigate through your first AI project. Through scraped knees, bruised elbows, and lessons learned from my AI deployments, I share with you the essentials so that you're successful in your journey. Thanks for taking this ride with me.

APPENDIX

Sources

Chapter 2

Figure 1: `https://spectrum.ieee.org/the-short-strange-life-of-the-first-friendly-robot`

History: `www.tableau.com/data-insights/ai/history`

Karel's poem: `www.gutenberg.org/files/59112/59112-h/59112-h.htm`

Giant Brains: `https://monoskop.org/images/b/bc/Berkeley_Edmund_Callis_Giant_Brains_or_Machines_That_Think.pdf`

Checkers: `https://en.wikipedia.org/wiki/Arthur_Samuel_(computer_scientist)`

Image of Unimate: `https://robotsguide.com/robots/unimate`

XCON: `https://en.wikipedia.org/wiki/Xcon#:~:text=XCON%20first%20went%20into%20use,achieved%2095%E2%80%9398%25%20accuracy`

Driver car Mercedes SEL: `www.politico.eu/article/delf-driving-car-born-1986-ernst-dickmanns-mercedes`

Chapter 3

Structured data: `https://aws.amazon.com/what-is/structured-data`

Advanced analytics: `https://aginic.com/blog/basic-vs-advanced-analytics#:~:text=While%20basic%20analytics%20focuses%20on,predict%20future%20trends%20and%20behaviours`

Descriptive model: `https://ceopedia.org/index.php/Descriptive_model`

Prescriptive models: `https://ceopedia.org/index.php/Analysis_of_information`

Predictive models: `https://cloud.google.com/learn/what-is-predictive-analytics#:~:text=Predictive%20analytics%20is%20the%20process,that%20might%20predict%20future%20behavior`

Pictures for desc/pred/pres: `www.mckinsey.com/capabilities/quantumblack/our-insights/an-executives-guide-to-ai`

Deep learning: `www.mckinsey.com/capabilities/quantumblack/our-insights/an-executives-guide-to-ai`

Unstructured data: `www.google.com/search?q=what+is+semi-structured+data&rlz=1C5GCEM_enUS1076US1076&oq=what+is+semi-st&gs_lcrp=EgZjaHJvbWUqBwgAEAAYgAQyBwgAEAAYgAQyBwgBEAAYgAQyBggCEEUYOTIHCAMQABiABDIHCAQQABiABDIHCAUQABiABDIHCAYQABiABDIICAcQABgWGB4yCAgIEAAYFhgeMggICRAAGBYYHqgCALACAA&sourceid=chrome&ie=UTF-8`

Data science: `www.ibm.com/topics/data-science`

Machine learning: `www.google.com/search?q=what+is+machine+learning&rlz=1C5GCEM_enUS1076US1076&oq=what+is+ma&gs_lcrp=EgZjaHJvbWUqDAgAEAAYQxiABBiKBTIMCAAQABhDGIAEGIoFMgwIARAAGAAQYYigUyBggCEEUYOTIHCAMQABiABDIKCAQQQABixAxiABDIKCAUQABixAxiABDIGCAYQRRg8MgYIBxBFGDyoAgCwAgA&sourceid=chrome&ie=UTF-8`

Chihuahua and blueberry muffin image: `www.facebook.com/Intelligen.au/photos/a.116360289910971/267901348090197/?type=3`

Neural networks: `www.ibm.com/topics/neural-networks`

Chapter 4

Industry annual value, McKinsey: www.mckinsey.com/
capabilities/quantumblack/our-insights/the-executives-ai-
playbook?page=industries

Robot harvesting cotton: www.mdpi.com/2624-7402/2/1/10

Robot in hazardous environment: www.atriainnovation.com/en/
la-robotica-colaborativa-en-entornos-peligrosos

The Jetsons: https://en.wikipedia.org/wiki/The_Jetsons

Research and development: IBM RXN https://rxn.res.ibm.com

Molecular modeling: www.atomwise.com/how-we-do-it

Index

A

AARON, 186
accountability
    approach to, 81
    as a tenet of responsible AI, 129–130
acquisition, 88
Adams, James L., 185
adjustments, 84
advertising, 149, 166
agriculture industry, impact of AI on, 143–144
agriculture robots, 144
AI. *See* artificial intelligence (AI)
AI boom, 185–186
AI Essentials Checklist, 72–74
AI literacy, future of AI for, 193
AI winter, 184–185
AI-powered stylists, 152
Alacritous Inc., 187
Alacrity, 187
algorithms, 138, 175
Alibaba, 188
aligning skillsets, 83
ambition, as a team virtue, 108
analytics, 176–179
Apple, 151, 188
approach
    about, 78–79
    on AI Essentials Checklist, 73, 74, 78–84
    change management, 79
    communication, 82–83
    ownership and accountability, 81
    project management, 78–79

staffing, 83–84
stakeholder identification, 81–82
talent training, 80
apps, 151
archetypes
    about, 107, 110–111
    Blind, 113
    Curmudgeon, 113
    Data Scientist, 114–115
    Discerner, 112–113
    Doer, 112
    Evangelist, 111–112
    Know-It All, 115
    Naysayer, 111
    Optimist, 114
    Saint, 114
artificial general intelligence (AGI), 196
artificial intelligence (AI). *See also*
    Responsible AI
    about, 169–170
    advances in, 196
    author's transition to, 18–21
    business benefits of, 7–8
    developing a strategy for, 28–30
    evolution of, 182–189
    framework for initiatives, 41–43
    future of, 191–199
    human intelligence compared with,
        172–173
    organizational benefits of, 6–7
    terminology, 173–182
    what it's not, 171–173

artificial super intelligence (ASI), 196
asking why, 27–28
audience, for communication, 82
automated email marketing, 166
automation, future of AI in, 191–192

B
bandwidth, impact on, 66
Bard, 189
Bechtel Corp., 141
Berkeley, Edmund Callis, 184
Blind archetype, 113
blue chips, impact of AI on, 140
Boston Consulting Group (BCG), 38
bots, 147
Breazeal, Cynthia, 187
budget, 87, 164
business benefits, of artificial intelligence
    (AI), 7–8
business growth, 8–9
business quotient (BQ), 22
business understanding, 44, 46–47, 52–53
business value, 75
businesses
    impact of AI on, 139–142
    as a layer of responsible AI, 127
business-to-business (B2B) sector, 94
BuzzFeed, 128–129

C
Canada Data and AI Act, 126
candidate sourcing, 159
Čapek, Karel, 183
Cargill, 141
Carpenter, Rollo, 187
case studies, in AI strategies, 60–61
categories, for establishing AI strategies, 44
CCPA, 130–131
change
    change management and, 118
    difficulties of, 105–107
    framework for, 26–35
change management
    about, 107, 115–118
    approach to, 79
    degree needed, 65
channels, of communication, 82
characters, 149
chatbots, 145, 147, 153, 159, 185
ChatGPT, 156, 169, 180, 186, 189
Chrysler, 141
Clearview AI, 131

clinical trials, 150
CNET, 128–129
code, 174–175
Cohen, Harold, 186
Coke, 153
communication
    approach to, 82–83
    change management and, 117
company culture
    about, 42, 44
    impact on, 65–66
    in readiness questionnaire, 48–49, 54
complexity, 63–64, 66–69
compliance monitoring, 157
computational power, of AI, 195
computer science
    about, 173
    algorithm, 175
    code, 174–175
    computer scientist, 173–174
    programming, 174
computer scientist, 173–174
computing power, 138
Conducting Readiness Assessment phase,
    42, 43–45
consequences, handling unintended, 87
consultants, future of AI for, 192
consumer electronics industry, impact of AI
    on, 150–151
content creation/moderation, 148–149
content generation/curation, 162–163
contract analysis, 157
contract review/analysis, 156
COPA, 130–131
crawlers, 147
Creating and Selecting Use Cases phase
    about, 42, 43, 61
    real-world and practical walk-through,
        69–72
    scoring criticality and complexity of use
        cases, 64–69
    use-case ideation, 61–63
    use-case selection, 63–64
criticality, 63–66
Criticality *vs.* Complexity Quadrant, 63–64
cross-functional impacts, 77–78
C-suite, 22
culture, company, 42
Curmudgeon archetype, 113
customer calls/follow-ups, 161
customer service function, impact of AI on,
    159–160
cybersecurity, AI and, 195

D

DALL-E, 188
data
   about, 44, 176
   AI and, 195
   in readiness questionnaire, 50–51, 55
data engineering, 176
data explosion, 138
data safeguards, 77
data science, 179
Data Scientist archetype, 114–115
data sources, 90–91
"day in the life," 88
The Day the Earth Stood Still (film), 182
Dean, Jeff, 188
decision-making, future of AI in, 192
deep learning (DL), 179, 185
deepfakes, 149
defined KPIs, 75
definition, change management and, 116
Deploying and Going Live phase, 42, 43,
   99–103
descriptive analytics, 177
developing AI strategies, 28–30
Dickman, Ernst, 187
digital divide, 131
directly catering to consumers (D2C), 94
Discerner archetype, 112–113
disease diagnosis/predictions, 144, 150
diversity, as a tenet of responsible
   AI, 132
Diversity & Non-Discrimination Act
   in AI, 132
Doer archetype, 112
driverless car, 187
Dropbox, 174
dynamic pricing, 145

E

E-discovery, 156
education chatbots, 153
education industry, impact of AI on,
   152–153
Effectiveness Strategy,
   29, 57, 59
Efficiency Strategy, 29, 56, 59
ELIZA, 184
emission control, 155
emotional quotient (EQ), 22
employment, impact of AI on, 193
end-state vision, 75
enhanced gaming experience, 148

enterprise, as a layer of responsible AI,
   126–127
enterprise integration, 89–90
environment health and safety (EHS)
   industry, impact of AI on, 154–155
Ernst & Young (E&Y), 21–22
Estee Lauder, 22
estimating projects, 34–35
ethical AI, future of AI for, 192, 193
ethical considerations, AI and, 195
ethical controversy, 77
EU AI Act, 126
evaluations, 84
Evangelist archetype, 111–112
evolution, of artificial intelligence (AI),
   182–189
expediting clinical trials, 150
expense categorization, 164
experience, 38–41
Experience and Willing, in will/skill
   matrix, 109
Expert Strategy, 29, 57–58, 59
experts, interoperability with, 92, 98–99

F

facial recognition (FR), 145, 180
fairness, as a tenet of responsible AI, 130
fashion and apparel
   industry, impact of AI on, 151–152
feedback, 82
finance function, impact of AI on, 163–164
financial planning and analysis
   (FP&A), 164
food and beverage industry, impact of AI
   on, 153–154
Food and Drug Administration (FDA), 188
food safety monitoring, 154
formats, for communication, 82
foundational pillars, 35–36
framework
   for AI initiatives, 41–43
   for change, 26–35
friend zone, 140
functioning prototype (FP), 85–86
functions, effect of AI on, 155–167

G

Gakutensoku robot, 183
Gamma App, 96
Gasparvo, Gary, 187
Gato, 188
GEMINI, 181, 189

General Data Protection Regulation (GDPR), 128, 130–131
General Motors, 185
generative AI, 21
getting started
    about, 37–38
    Conducting Readiness Assessments phase, 43–55
    Creating and Selecting Use Cases phase, 61–72
    Deploying and Going Live phase, 99–103
    experience, 38–41
    framework for AI initiatives, 41–43
    Preparing and Designing phase, 72–91
    Selecting a Solution phase, 91–99
    Selecting an AI strategy phase, 55–61
Giant Brains or Machines that Think (Berkeley), 184
Gladwell, Malcolm, 82
go-live support, 89
Google, 174, 188, 189
Google Drive, 174
governance, future of AI for, 192
governments, as a layer of responsible AI, 126
GPT, 180
grit, as a team virtue, 108
growth, impact on, 64–65
Growth Strategy, 30, 58, 59

H

Harvard Business Review, 38
hazard identification, 154
healthcare industry
    future of AI for, 193
    impact of AI on, 149–150
Herzberg, Elaine, 129–130
higher education, 153
Higson, Ralph, 170
human in the loop
    about, 123–124, 132–133
    example of, 133–136
    Responsible AI, 124–132
human intelligence (HI), 172–173
human resources (HR) function, impact of AI on, 158–159

I

I, Robot (film), 182
IBM, 20, 187, 188
IBM 701, 184

IBM Watson, 20–21, 188
iCloud, 174
IKEA, 141
impacts
    about, 76–77, 137
    on agriculture industry, 143–144
    on AI Essentials Checklist, 73, 74, 76–78
    on blue chips, 140
    on businesses, 139–142
    on consumer electronics industry, 150–151
    cross-functional, 77–78
    on customer service function, 159–160
    on education industry, 152–153
    on environment health and safety industry, 154–155
    ethical controversy, 77
    on fashion and apparel industry, 151–152
    on finance function, 163–164
    on food and beverage industry, 153–154
    on functions, 155–167
    on healthcare industry, 149–150
    on human resources function, 158–159
    on industries, 143–155
    on legal function, 156
    on manufacturing industry, 145–146
    on marketing function, 166
    on media and entertainment industry, 148–149
    partnerships, 78
    PR, 77
    on procurement function, 156–157
    on project management office function, 157–158
    on research and development function, 164–165
    on retail industry, 146–147
    safeguards on data, 77
    on sales function, 161–162
    on scale-ups, 141–142
    on small business operations, 141
    on small businesses, 142
    on start-ups, 141–142
    tipping point for AI, 138–139
    on training and development function, 162–163
    on travel and leisure industry, 145
    on well-off private companies, 140–141
inclusiveness, as a tenet of responsible AI, 131
individuals, as a layer of responsible AI, 127–128
industries, impact of AI on, 143–155

inertia, overcoming, 3–5
Inexperience but Willing, in will/skill
    matrix, 109
influencers, 149
inspections, 146, 154
Instagram, 174
insurance laws, future of AI for, 194
intelligent quotient (IQ), 22
intelligent training systems, 162
interactive skill development, 163
interoperability, with experts, 92, 98–99
investments, change management and, 116
Investopedia, 38
The Invisible Boy (film), 182
involvement, change management and, 117
iteration, change management and, 117
Ivakhnenko, Alexey, 185

J
Jabberwocky, 187
Jennings, Ken, 188

K
key messages, 82
key performance indicators (KPIs), 75, 83
Know-It-All archetype, 115
knowledge base, 160

L
language learning, 153
large language models (LLMs), 94
leadership alignment, change management
    and, 116–117
learning platforms, 153
legal function, impact of AI on, 156
legal research, 156
liability laws, future of AI for, 194
List Processing (LISP), 185
Logic Theorist, 184

M
machine learning (ML)
    about, 178–179, 185
    AI and, 195
    future of, 191
maintenance support, 89
management consulting, future of
    AI in, 192
manifesto, change management and, 116
manufacturing industry, impact of AI on,
    145–146

market strategy, 44, 45–46, 51–52
marketing function, impact of AI on, 166
Mars, 141
material science, 165
McCarthy, John, 184, 185
McKinsey, 143
media and entertainment industry, impact
    of AI on, 148–149
medicine, 150
mental health, future of AI for, 194
Merck Pharmaceuticals, 22
Meta, 130, 188
metrics, approach to, 83
Metropolis (film), 182
Minimum Viable Product (MVP), 85
mobile device management (MDM), 19
molecular modeling, 165
monitoring, change management and, 117
multiplier effect, 34, 35
music composition, 149

N
NASA, 187
natural language processing (NLP), 21,
    180, 192
Naysayer archetype, 111
net promoter scores (NPSs), 58
neural networks (NNs), 179–180, 188
Ng, Andrew, 188
Nishimura, Makoto, 183
nondiscrimination, as a tenet of responsible
    AI, 132

O
objectives, setting, 82
OpenAI, 169, 186, 188, 189
operations, impact on, 65
Optimist archetype, 114
optimizing reaction conditions, 165
Optum, 132
organizational benefits, of artificial
    intelligence (AI), 6–7
outsourcing, 45
ownership
    approach to, 81
    change management and, 116
    of use cases, 67–69
ownership of code, 87

P
pacing yourself, 32–35
PaLM, 188

partnerships, 78
people challenges
   about, 105
   AI archetypes, 107, 110–115
   change, 105–107
   change management, 107, 115–118
   example of, 118–122
   team virtues, 106, 107–110
performance expectations,
   86–87
perpetual POC purgatory, 140
personal style, 41
personalization at scale, future of AI for,
   192
personalized learning, 153
personalized medicine, 150
personalized recommendations, 147
personalized sales messages, 162
pest detection, AI in, 144
post-meeting notes, 71
PR, bad, 77
precision farming, AI in, 144
predictive analytics, 177
predictive manufacturing, 146
predictive recommendations, 159
Preparing and Designing phase
   about, 42, 43, 72–74
   approach, 78–84
   impacts, 76–78
   process, 84–88
   support, 89–91
   vision, 74–76
prescriptive analytics,
   177–178
presentation creation, 71
privacy, as a tenet of responsible AI,
   130–131
process
   about, 84–85
   acquisition, 88
   on AI Essentials Checklist, 73, 74, 84–88
   budget, 87
   "day in the life," 88
   functioning prototype (FP), 85–86
   handling unintended consequences, 87
   Minimum Viable Product (MVP), 85
   ownership of code, 87
   performance expectations, 86–87
   procurement, 88
   proof of concept (POC), 86
   workflows, 88
procurement function, impact of AI on, 89,
   156–157

Productivity Strategy, 29, 57, 59
programmatic advertising, 166
programming, 174
project estimation, 34–35
project management (PM), approach to, 79
project management office (PMO) function,
   impact of AI on, 157–158
prompt engineering, 181–182
proof of concept (POC), 31, 86
psychology, future of AI
   for, 194
public perception, impact on, 65–66
Python language, 175

Q
quality, 90–91, 154
quality control, 146
quality monitoring, 154

R
Rashidi, Solmaz (author)
   about, 15, 133
   formative years of, 14–18
   as rogue executive, 12–14
   sports for, 16–18
   transition to artificial intelligence (AI),
      18–21
reaction conditions, 165
readiness questionnaire, 45–55
research and development (R&D) function,
   impact of AI on, 164–165
resilience, as a team virtue, 108
resource allocation models, 158
Responsible AI
   about, 124–125
   accountability, 129–130
   diversity, 132
   fairness, 130
   inclusiveness, 131
   layers of responsibility, 125–128
   nondiscrimination, 132
   privacy, 130–131
   tenets of, 128–132
   transparency, 128–129
résumé screening, 159
retail industry, impact of AI on, 146–147
retrospectives, change management and,
   117
risk mitigation process, 91
risk prediction/management, 158
robot-assisted surgery, 150
robotics, 144, 146

"rogue executive", 11–14
role of technology, 44, 49–50, 54
Roomba, 151, 187
route availability, 145
Royal Caribbean, 22
Rutter, Brad, 188

S

Saint archetype, 114
sales function, impact of AI on, 64–65,
    161–162
sales presentations, 161–162
Samuel, Arthur, 183, 184
scale-ups, impact of AI on, 141–142
scaling
    future of AI for, 193–194
    speed of, 30–31
scope, 75–76
scoring, 64–69
search engine optimization (SEO), 166
security measures, 90
security systems, future of AI for, 193
Selecting a Solution phase
    about, 42, 43, 91–92
    interoperability with experts, 92, 98–99
    tool selection, 92–97
Selecting an AI Strategy phase
    about, 42, 55–56
    case studies, 60–61
    Effectiveness Strategy,
        57, 59
    Efficiency Strategy, 56, 59
    Expert Strategy, 57–58, 59
    Growth Strategy, 58, 59
    Productivity Strategy,
        57, 59
semi-structured data, 176
sentiment analysis, 160
Siri, 188
skills gap, AI and, 195
skillset, aligning, 83
small, starting, 30–31
small business operations
    future of AI for, 194
    impact of AI on, 141, 142
smart home devices, 151
smart speakers, 151
smart TVs, 151
smartphones, 151
social quotient (SQ), 22
solicitation, 82
solutions, AI, 94–96

Sony Music, 22
specialization, 84
speed
    of AI, 194–195
    of scaling, 30–31
sports, for author, 16–18
Sports Illustrated,
    128–129
SQL language, 174–175
staffing model, 83–84
stakeholder identification, approach to,
    81–82
Standford Cart, 185
Star Trek (film), 182
Star Wars (film), 182
start-ups, impact of AI on, 141–142
strategy, developing for AI, 28–30
structured data, 176
support
    about, 89
    on AI Essentials Checklist,
        73, 74, 89–91
    approach to, 83
    data sources, 90–91
    enterprise integration,
        89–90
    go-live support, 89
    maintenance support, 89
    quality, 90–91
    risk mitigation process, 91
    security measures, 90
    systems, 90–91
sustainable development,
    future of AI for, 193
sustainable fashion, 152
systems, 90–91

T

talent training, approach
    to, 80
targeted advertising, 149
task automation, 158
team virtues, 106, 107–110
teams
    building, 83
    dynamics of, 84
    inheriting, 83
technology
    choosing partners, 31–35
    future of AI for integrating,
        192
terminology, 173–182

Tesla, 151
thinking big, 30–31
time commitment, 40
tools
    AI, 94–96
    selecting, 92–97
training, approach to, 83
training and development (T&D) function,
    impact of AI on, 162–163
transition, change management and, 117
transparency, as a tenet of responsible AI,
    128–129
travel and leisure industry, impact of AI on,
    145
trend predictions, 152
triaging, 160
Turing, Alan, 183, 184
Turing test, 184

U
Uber, 129–130
Unimate robot, 185
unstructured data, 176
Unwilling with Experience, in will/skill
    matrix, 109
Unwilling with No Experience, in will/
    skill matrix, 109
use-case ideation, 61–63
use-case selection, 61,
    63–64

V
vendor risk management,
    157

victories, change management and, 117
virtual agents, 145
virtual try-ons, 147
vision
    on AI Essentials Checklist,
        73, 74–76
    business value, 75
    defined KPIs, 75
    defined scope, 75–76
    end-state, 75
    setting, 82
    the "why," 74–75
voice assistants, 151

W
waste reduction, 154
Watson (IBM), 20–21, 188
wearables, 150, 155
website optimization, 166
Weizenbaum, Joseph, 185
well-off private companies, impact of AI
    on, 140–141
the "why," 27–28, 74–75
will/skill matrix, 106,
    108–110
workflows, 88
workforce acumen, 44, 47–48, 53

X
XCON, 186

Y
yourself, pacing, 32–35